The Stewart English Program

Book 3
Writing Plus...

Donald S. Stewart

About the author: Donald S. Stewart taught English at Belmont Hill School, an independent school for boys in Belmont, Massachusetts. In 1990 he founded Write for College, an intensive summer writing course that he directed for 25 years, preparing high school students from the Boston area for the writing challenges of college and beyond. In 2015 he took the course online at http://writingwhatever.com.

Published by BookLocker.com, Inc., St. Petersburg, Florida.

Printed on acid-free paper.

BookLocker.com, Inc.
2018

Second edition

Cover designed by Shar www.fiverr.com/landofawes

CONTENTS

INTRODUCTION

I have always been intrigued by the question put to me years ago by a colleague, a biology teacher. "What animals," he asked, "were the last to learn about the ocean?" Birds, he then explained, knew about the ocean because they had seen it from the air. The creatures dwelling on land knew about it because they had walked along the shore. But because they were immersed in it, living in it and breathing it, the animals that learned last about the sea that surrounded them, that touched them every moment of their lives, were the fish.

We are like those fish, and the sea we swim in is our English language. We are born into it, frolic in it, occasionally get lost in it, and grow in it. And finally there comes the time when we begin to learn about it. We learn the names of the parts, how those parts work together, and how to make them work for us. That is why this series is called *Principles Plus*, *Grammar Plus*, and *Writing Plus*.

I wish to express my indebtedness to the late Francis Christensen and his wife, Bonniejean, for the inspiration for these textbooks. *Writing Plus*, the third in the series, is my revision of their masterpiece, *The Christensen Rhetoric Program*, which proved beyond a doubt that writing can be taught actively, not just reactively. Their method, of observation, discovery, and assimilation, is the most natural of learning styles for the young people who stand at the threshold of opportunity and responsibility as the writers of the future.

May I also thank the many students I taught at Belmont Hill School over the years, for their encouragement, their enthusiasm in collecting the sample sentences from their favorite books, and their willingness to be the most honest of critics as I refined my presentation. The sparkle in their eyes has been my greatest reward.

—Donald S. Stewart

1. MODIFIERS

To begin this writing course, let us look at an observation made by John Erskine, the founder of the *Great Books* series, a practicing novelist, and a teacher of writing. It is an interesting piece of advice, especially when you consider how often we are told to keep our sentences lean and our nouns and verbs powerful and unadorned.

> When you write, you make a point, not by subtracting as though you sharpened a pencil, but by adding. . . . The noun, the verb, and the main clause serve merely as a base on which the meaning will rise. . . . The modifier is the essential part of any sentence.

Imagine that you are at a party and that a friend wants to introduce her cousin to you. She points to a group of people standing by the punch bowl and says, "There he is."

You aren't quite sure whom she means, so you ask, "Which one?"

"He's the tall boy with the green Irish sweater."

Now you know which one is her cousin. The added modifiers *tall* and *with the green Irish sweater* helped you pick him out of the crowd.

THE FIRST PRINCIPLE: ADDITION

The first principle of all writing is the principle of **addition**. It is by adding modifiers—adjectives and adverbs, phrases and clauses—that we make our general ideas more vivid and specific.

In the situation above, the modifiers *tall* and *with the green Irish sweater* we will call **bound modifiers** because they are in fixed positions in the sentence and are not separated from what they are modifying, *boy,* by any mark of punctuation.

In contrast to bound modifiers, **free modifiers** are set off from the main clause by some form of punctuation, usually a comma. We will call the main clause the **base clause,** as it is the base upon which we will build our ideas.

> She met him at the appointed time in the Plaza lobby, a lovely, faded, gray-eyed blonde in a coat of Russian sable. — F. Scott Fitzgerald

Here, the pronoun *She,* the first word in the sentence, is being modified. The free modifier is *a lovely, faded, gray-eyed blonde in a coat of Russian sable.* Notice that it is at the opposite end of the sentence, set off by a comma.

You should also notice, by the way, that the commas between *lovely, faded,* and *gray-eyed* do not set off free modifiers, but rather separate adjectives (bound modifiers) leading up to the noun *blonde.*

So far, we have shown how a noun and a pronoun may be modified by bound or free modifiers. The principle of addition also allows us to clarify an action expressed in the verb.

> The picadors galloped jerkily around the ring. — Ernest Hemingway

Here the verb *galloped* is modified by the adverb *jerkily,* which tells the manner of the action, and by the prepositional phrase *around the ring,* which tells place. These are bound modifiers, attached directly to the verb in relatively fixed positions.

Now look at a sentence that adds free modifiers to help capture the excitement of a fishing trip.

We caught two bass, hauling them in quickly as though they were mackerel, pulling them over the side of the boat in a businesslike manner without any landing net, and stunning them with a blow on the back of the head. — E. B. White

Each of the free modifiers in this sentence is a participial phrase, beginning with a present participle—*hauling, pulling, stunning*—followed by the necessary complements and bound modifiers, which add more details. While these participial phrases modify the subject *we*, they also develop the idea proposed in the verb *caught*. Such is the nature of free modifiers, that they often serve more as sentence modifiers than as word modifiers.

It is interesting to observe that the base clause above contains only four words, while the free modifiers total thirty-seven. Again, as John Erskine noted, **"The modifier is the essential part of any sentence."**

We will not be much concerned in this course with bound modifiers, because they offer little possibility of manipulation and usually just take care of themselves. Free modifiers, however, offer virtually unlimited stylistic potential.

POSITION OF FREE MODIFIERS

In the sentences you have seen by F. Scott Fitzgerald and E.B. White, the free modifiers were written after the main clause. Such a sentence is called a **cumulative sentence,** because the modifiers are added, or *accumulate,* after the base clause, providing details or explaining the action.

Free modifiers may also be placed before the base clause or within it. To show the relationship between the base clause and the free modifier more clearly, we will number the base clause as a **Level 1** and the free modifier as an indented **Level 2**. If the free modifier falls within the Level 1, we use the slant symbol (/) to show the interruption, and the Level 2 is now identified as a **2/**. Here are three examples that show free modifiers in the initial, medial, or final positions.

initial position
      2   Living in the mountains,
  1   I eat fish every chance I get and wonder what the sea is like.
                      —Doris Betts

medial position
  1   She wore a pale pink crepe de Chine frock, /, and a matching silk
        hair ribbon tying back her pale soft curls.
     2/ smocked around the yoke with rose
                    —Carson McCullers

final position
  1   We rode on up to our big gate,
      2   where my father dismounted to open it and let me myself ride
      Nellie Gray through.   —Robert Penn Warren

THE SECOND PRINCIPLE: LEVELS OF GENERALITY

We have said that the first principle of the cumulative sentence is the principle of addition. The second principle is called **levels of generality**. As the sentence adds free modifiers, moving from general observations to specific details, it develops a rhythm and a flow, which we may continue to number. As we noted earlier, a Level 2 free modifier expands on what has been said in the Level 1 base clause, modifying a noun, the verb, or even the entire sentence. A Level 3 will modify something in the Level 2, a Level 4 will modify something in the Level 3, and so on. Only the Level 1 will be a complete sentence; all other levels are free modifiers.

> Joad's lips stretched tight over his long teeth for a moment, and he licked his lips, like a dog, two licks, one in each direction from the middle. — John Steinbeck

> 1 Joad's lips stretched tight over his long teeth for a moment, and
> 1 he licked his lips,
>   2 like a dog,
>   3 two licks,
>   4 one in each direction from the middle.

One must admire John Steinbeck's persistence in staying with this comparison until he had it just right. Knowing that Tom Joad licked his lips *like a dog* is helpful, but it is still too general to bring the action into sharp focus. Moving another level down, *two licks,* gets us closer, but there are still too many ways that the motion might happen. Only when we know that the movement is *one in each direction from the middle* can we stick out our tongues and do it ourselves. Steinbeck must have watched dozens of dogs eating hundreds of dog bones before he got the phrasing just right!

> Then I saw the dark muzzle and the shadow of horns, and then, with a clattering on the wood in the hollow box, the bull charged and came out into the corral, skidding with his forefeet in the straw as he stopped, his head up, the great hump of muscle on his neck swollen tight, his body muscles quivering as he looked up at the crowd on the stone walls. — Ernest Hemingway

> 1 Then I saw the dark muzzle and the shadow of horns, and
> 1 then, / , the bull charged and came out into the corral,
>   2/ with a clattering on the wood in the hollow box
>   2 skidding with his forefeet in the straw as he stopped,
>   3 his head up,
>   3 the great hump of muscle on his neck swollen tight,
>   3 his body muscles quivering as he looked up at the crowd on the stone walls.

Here there are two Level 1s, each an independent clause, joined by a coordinating conjunction. The second Level 1 is interrupted by a Level 2, as shown by the slant. Another Level 2 then follows the second Level 1, and it in turn is followed by three consecutive Level 3s. Try reading just the two Level 1s. We know what happened, but we get little sense of the sounds or the magnificent fierceness of the bull. The power of the image comes directly from the free modifiers.

Here are several more examples of sentences by professional writers that show how to use free modifiers, in their various positions.

Base clauses with initial and/or final modifiers only

> The voices made a single, steady noise in the room, a noise without words, rising and falling but still steady, coming at a man like waves and washing upon him.
> — A. B. Guthrie, Jr.

1   The voices made a single, steady noise in the room,
    2   a noise without words,
        3   rising and falling but still steady,
        3   coming at a man like waves and washing upon him.

Slenderly, languidly, their hands set lightly on their hips, the two young women preceded us out onto a rosy-colored porch, open toward the sunlight, where four candles flickered on the table in the diminished wind.   — F. Scott Fitzgerald

    2   Slenderly,
    2   languidly,
    2   their hands set lightly on their hips,
1   the two young women preceded us out onto a rosy-colored porch,
    2   open toward the sunlight,
    2   where four candles flickered on the table in the diminished wind.

Letting in a clutch is a negative, hesitant motion, depending on delicate nervous control; pushing down the Ford pedal was a simple, country motion—an expansive act, which came as natural as kicking an old door to make it budge.
                —E. B. White

1   Letting in a clutch is a negative, hesitant motion,
    2   depending on delicate nervous control;
1   pushing down the Ford pedal was a simple, country motion—
    2   an expansive act,
        3   which came as natural as kicking an old door to make it budge.

Across his nose, from left to right, he dragged the sleeve of his Davy Crockett jerkin, leaving the mica-like trail of a snail on his cuff.   —Wright Morris

    2   Across his nose,
        3   from left to right,
1   he dragged the sleeve of his Davy Crockett jerkin,
    2   leaving the mica-like trail of a snail on his cuff.

Nineteen years old, six feet two inches tall, long of bone and hard of muscle, with sunburned faces and auburn hair, their eyes merry and arrogant, their bodies clothed in identical blue coats and mustard-colored breeches, they were as much alike as two bolls of cotton.   —Margaret Mitchell

    2   Nineteen years old,
    2   six feet two inches tall,
    2   long of bone and hard of muscle,
    2   with sunburned faces and auburn hair,
    2   their eyes merry and arrogant,
    2   their bodies clothed in identical blue coats and mustard-colored
            breeches,
1   they were as much alike as two bolls of cotton.

He sat by John Thornton's fire, a broad-breasted dog, white-fanged and long-furred; but behind him were the shades of all manner of dogs, half-wolves and wild wolves, urgent and prompting, tasting the savor of the meat he ate, thirsting for the water he drank, scenting the wind with him, listening with him and telling him the sounds made by the wild life in the forest, dictating his moods, directing his actions, lying down to sleep with him when he lay down, and dreaming with him and beyond him and becoming themselves the stuff of his dreams. — Jack London

    1   He sat by John Thornton's fire,
        2   a broad-breasted dog,
            3   white-fanged and long-furred; but
    1   behind him were the shades of all manner of dogs,
        2   half-wolves and wild wolves,
            3   urgent and prompting,
            3   tasting the savor of the meat he ate,
            3   thirsting for the water he drank,
            3   scenting the wind with him,
            3   listening with him and telling him the sounds made by the wild
                life in the forest,
            3   dictating his moods,
            3   directing his actions,
            3   lying down to sleep with him when he lay down, and
            3   dreaming with him and beyond him and becoming themselves
                the stuff of his dreams.

Base clauses with medial modifiers

Granmom's eyes, worn bits of crazed crystal embedded in watery milk, widened behind her cockeyed spectacles.   — John Updike

    1   Granmom's eyes, /, widened behind her cockeyed spectacles.
        2/ worn bits of crazed crystal embedded in watery milk

Miss Buell's face, which was old and greyish and kindly, with gray stiff curls beside the cheeks and eyes that swam very brightly, like little minnows behind thick glasses, wrinkled itself into a complication of amusement.   — Conrad Aiken

    1   Miss Buell's face, /, wrinkled itself into a complication of amusement.
        2/ which was old and greyish and kindly,
            3   with gray stiff curls beside the cheeks and eyes that swam
                very brightly,
                4   like little minnows behind thick glasses

Regina Cartwright, guiding her white horse down the path from the stables to the drive, careful of the surrounding flowers, could see that the bedroom curtains were still drawn.   — Antonia Fraser

    1   Regina Cartwright, /, could see that the bedroom curtains were still drawn.
        2/ guiding her white horse down the path from the stables to the drive,
            3   careful of the surrounding flowers

MODIFIERS

Name:_____

EXERCISE A: free modifiers and levels of generality

Accuracy_____

Directions: Rewrite the following sentences using numbers to indicate the various levels of generality, indenting where necessary. Note that the separating commas between coordinate adjectives (as after *pale* in item 6 and *worn* in item 8) do not mark free modifiers. There may be more blank lines for you to write on than there are levels in the sentence, since some levels may need two blank lines.

1. Mothers with babies, fathers holding up young children, couples arm in arm, boys toting roller skates and baseball bats, European tourists in berets—all stood motionless and silent.
    —E. B. White

_____

_____

_____

_____

_____

_____

2. Her thin figure, seated stiffly upright, arms against her sides, the legs close together, the shoulders square, the head upright, is like that of an Egyptian statue. —Eugene O'Neill

_____

_____

_____

_____

_____

_____

3. I had been visiting her flat for years before I noticed two long shelves of books, under a window, each shelf filled with the works of a single writer. —Doris Lessing

_____

_____

_____

_____

4. She was mending a large, long table-cloth of the finest texture, holding it up against the light occasionally to discover thin places, which required her delicate care. —Elizabeth Gaskell

_____

_____

_____

5. Someone was coming toward me along the bent, broken lane which led to the dormitory, a lane out of old London, ancient houses on either side leaning as though soon to tumble into it, cobblestones heaving underfoot like a bricked-over ocean squall. —John Knowles

_____

_____

_____

_____

_____

6. The minister, a pale, feeble-looking man with white hair and blond chin-whiskers, took his seat beside the small table and placed his Bible upon it. —Willa Cather

_____

_____

_____

_____

7. Nine antelope in loose file, with silently flagging fawns, came on trigger toe up the meadow and drank at the well, heads often up, muzzles dripping, broad ears turning. —Walter Van Tilburg Clark

8. On the table a book lay, a Bible, an ordinary kind of Bible with worn, imitation leather covers. —Robert Penn Warren

9. Mrs. Morse lay on her back, one flabby, white arm flung up, the wrist against her forehead. —Dorothy Parker

10. He hurried through the last words, shut the book, and then fell backwards against the door, gap- toothed, staring at the enormous, shapeless figure that stood within the pentagram, lit only by the blue flicker of its waving, fiery claws. —Ursula LeGuin

---

---

11. When Miss Emily Grierson died, our whole town went to her funeral: the men through a sort of respectful affection for a fallen monument, the women mostly out of curiosity to see the inside of her house, which no one save an old manservant—a combined gardener and cook—had seen in at least ten years.
—William Faulkner

2. THE VERB PHRASE

You probably noticed from the exercises you have done so far that there are several kinds of free modifiers, from simple adjectives and adverbs, to more elaborate phrases and clauses. In the next five chapters, we will take a closer look at these free modifiers and practice using them to make our writing more interesting and specific.

The first free modifier we will consider is the **verb phrase**. A verb phrase consists of a verbal (present participle, past participle, or infinitive) with accompanying complements and modifiers.

PRESENT PARTICIPIAL PHRASE AS MODIFIER

The present participle form of the verb is made by adding -*ing* to the infinitive, occasionally with a slight spelling modification: *talk/talking, be/being, win/winning, take/taking*.

By using the present participle form, we can create the progressive tenses.

(past progressive)	The clown *was juggling* two tennis balls and a bowling ball.
(present progressive)	Some students *are building* a snow sculpture for the carnival.
(future progressive)	The parade *will be honoring* the veterans on Memorial Day.

By removing the helping verbs (*was, are, will be*), we are left with nouns and **present participial phrases**, which serve as adjectives modifying the nouns.

> The clown *juggling two tennis balls and a bowling ball* was the hit of the circus.
> The students *building a snow sculpture for the carnival* came in for hot chocolate.
> The parade *honoring the veterans on Memorial Day* will depart from the town hall.

These present participial phrases would be considered bound modifiers, because they are not set off from the nouns they modify by commas. They are sometimes called **restrictive phrases**, because they are necessary to narrow down, limit, or restrict the noun from a larger number of possibilities. There were probably several clowns at the circus. Not all students were building the snow sculpture. This was one special parade.

When verb phrases modify a noun in the sentence other than the subject, they are almost always **restrictive**, even if the noun is quite specific. Here are two examples.

> We watched the blacksmith *demonstrating how to shape the horseshoe.*
> The proud parents took several pictures of their daughter *taking her first steps.*

When the phrase is a free modifier, however, and therefore set apart from the base clause by a comma or commas, it would be **nonrestrictive**. The identity of the noun would already be apparent from the context, so it would not be necessary to restrict, or narrow down, the possibilities.

In Chapter 1 you learned that free modifiers may often go in more than one location in the sentence. Here is how a sentence that contains the present participle form of the verb, along with a complement *(the caves)* and a prepositional phrase modifier *(along the coast),* may provide a present participial phrase as a free modifier.

(original sentence)	The scientists were *exploring the caves along the coast.*
(initial position)	*Exploring the caves along the coast,* the scientists discovered several artifacts from a prehistoric settlement.
(medial position)	The scientists, *exploring the caves along the coast,* were almost stranded by the incoming tide.
(final position)	The scientists spent nearly a month in Oregon, *exploring the caves along the coast.*

Here is a reconstruction of a sentence by Walter Van Tilburg Clark, describing the movements of a hawk.

He [the hawk] could sail for hours.
He searched the blanched grasses below him with his telescopic eye.
He gained height against the wind.
He descended in mile-long, gently declining swoops when he curved and rode back.
He never beat a wing.

Written as a five-sentence paragraph, this attempt to describe the graceful movement of the bird is choppy and repetitious, not at all in keeping with the image or feeling it is trying to convey.

Here is how the author actually pictured the scene:

1 He [the hawk] could sail for hours,
2 *searching* the blanched grasses below him with his telescopic eye,
2 *gaining* height against the wind,
2 *descending* in mile-long, gently declining swoops when he curved and rode back,
2 *never beating* a wing.

The Level 1 is unchanged from the topic sentence we created above. But by using the present participial forms of the verbs, rather than writing four more sentences, Clark captured the grace and rhythm of the hawk's flight, moving from the general verb *sail* into four of its components in the lower levels.

Here is another example showing free modifiers based on present participles, this time describing the movements of water from a spring.

2 In its basin there,
1 the perfectly clear water eddied ceaselessly,
2 *braiding* and *swelling,*
2 *swaying* the young fronds of fern and the grass which trailed lushly down to the surface,
2 *spilling* over the lip of stone, and
2 *plunging* down the slope to join the creek below.
—Robert Penn Warren

PAST PARTICIPIAL PHRASE AS MODIFIER

Regular verbs form the **past participle** by adding *-ed* to the infinitive, perhaps with a slight alteration of spelling: *clean/cleaned, type/typed, omit/omitted.*

Irregular verbs form the past participle in a number of different ways: *write/written, drink/drunk, be/been, lead/led, make/made, split /split.*

The past participle form of the verb is used to create the perfect tenses.

(past perfect)	The painters *had finished* the house but not the garage.
(present perfect)	My parents *have gone* away for the weekend.
(future perfect)	By Friday we *will have delivered* the last pages to the publisher.

The past participle form of the verb is also used to create the passive voice.

(past perfect, passive)	The notice *had been hung* on the bulletin board.
(present perfect, passive)	The documents *have been filed* for safekeeping.
(future perfect, passive)	By sundown the trucks *will have been loaded* for market.

It is the passive voice that provides us with the **past participial phrase** we will use as a modifier. By removing the helping verbs *(had been, have been, will have been),* we are left with past participial phrases modifying the subjects.

The notice *hung on the bulletin board* announced her candidacy for class president.
The documents *filed for safekeeping* contain the addresses of all the employees.
The trucks *loaded for market* will leave as soon as the rear doors are closed.

Like the present participial phrases, past participial phrases may be either restrictive or nonrestrictive. As nonrestrictive phrases, they are free modifiers and may often be placed in more than one position in the sentence.

(original sentence)	The audience was *thrilled with the violinist's performance.*
(initial position)	*Thrilled with the violinist's performance*, the audience gave her a standing ovation.
(medial position)	The audience, *thrilled with the violinist's performance*, shouted for more.
(final position)	The audience reluctantly left the concert hall, *thrilled with the violinist's performance.*

Here are three sentences that illustrate the use of the past participial phrase as a free modifier.

1   Further on was a cement sidewalk,
    2   *ruled* into geometrical parallelograms,
    2   with a brassy inlay at one end commemorating the contractors who had laid it, and, halfway across, an irregular and random series of dog tracks,
       3   *immortalized* in synthetic stone. —Conrad Aiken

1   His eyes were light blue and lashless,
    2   bulging slightly,
    2   *rimmed* with pink,
    2   *magnified* behind large, watery spectacles whose clear frames had an unfortunate pinkish cast themselves. —Anne Tyler

1   A strong smell of scent emanated from her many pleats and folds, and
1   Mother's famous diamond earrings were in place,
    2   *touched* from time to time by fingers with long scarlet nails.
               —Anita Brookner

INFINITIVE PHRASE AS MODIFIER

The infinitive is the form you would use to look up a verb in a dictionary. As a modifier it will usually begin with the word *to: to sing, to cover, to become, to travel, to be.* An **infinitive phrase** may contain its own complements and modifiers.

As a bound modifier, an infinitive phrase often modifies a verb, answering the question *Why?*

> We bought twenty yards of black cloth *to make our Halloween costumes.*

An infinitive phrase may also modify an adjective or an adverb.

> The astronauts were happy *to get back to earth.*
> On our trip across the country, we traveled too fast *to enjoy all the wonderful sights.*

As a free modifier, the infinitive phrase will usually serve as an appositive, restating or explaining a noun in the previous level of generality.

1   Intuitively I've always been aware of the vitally important pact which a man has with himself,
     2   *to be* all things to himself, and
     2   *to be identified* with all things,
     2   *to stand* self-reliant,
         3   taking advantage of his haphazard connection with a planet,
         3   riding his luck, and
         3   following his bent with the tenacity of a hound. —E. B. White

THE VERB PHRASE

Name:_____

EXERCISE A: writing verb phrases

Accuracy_____

Directions: In each sentence, supply a verb phrase that uses the verb form called for—either a present participle, a past participle, or an infinitive. Feel free to expand the verb phrases by including well-chosen complements and modifiers.

1. 1   She dried the dishes carefully,

    2   _____.
                            (present participle)

2. 1   The lawn mower, / , wasn't worth repairing.

    2/ _____
                            (past participle)

3. 2   Since this was his first day in the new school,

    1   his attempts _____
                            (infinitive)

    irritated his classmates.

4. 1   People crowded the benches in the park,

    2   _____ .
                            (present participle)

5. 1   She walked off hurriedly down the road,

    2   _____ over her shoulder.
                            (present participle)

6. 1   On Saturday they did many things _____ :
                            (infinitive)

    2   _____ ,
                            (present participle)

    2   _____ , and
                            (present participle)

    2   _____ .
                            (present participle)

7. 1   The French tapestry, / , is the main attraction at the museum's most recent exhibit.

    2/ _____ .
                            (past participle)

15

8. 1   This was a perfect day to indulge one's fancies:

     2   _____ ,
                                    (infinitive)
     2   _____ , and
                                    (infinitive)
     2   _____ .
                                    (infinitive)

9. 1   They worked on the school yearbook enthusiastically,

     2   _____ and
                                (present participle)
     2   _____ .
                                (present participle)

10. 1   The castle, / was the last stop on our tour.

     2/   _____ .
                                    (past participle)

THE VERB PHRASE

Name:_____

EXERCISE B: more verb phrases

Accuracy _____ Creativity _____

Directions: The following exercise will give you further practice in the use of the verb phrase in slightly more complicated sentences. Feel free to expand the verb phrases by including well-chosen complements and modifiers.

1.　　2　_____,
　　　　　　　　　　　　　　　(present participle)

　　1　she was anxious _____ .
　　　　　　　　　　　　　　　(infinitive)

2.　1　He rushed past the crowd on the corner,

　　　2　a man too busy _____ .
　　　　　　　　　　　　　　(infinitive)

3 .　1　The cat, /, scrambled to the lowest branch of the pine.

　　　2/　_____
　　　　　　　　　　　　　　(past participle)

4.　1　They were looking for a place _____,
　　　　　　　　　　　　　　　(infinitive)

　　　2　somewhere _____ .
　　　　　　　　　　　　　　(infinitive)

5.　　2　After _____,
　　　　　　　　　　　　　　(present participle)

　　1　they expected _____ and _____ .
　　　　　　　　　　(infinitive)　　　　　　　　　*(infinitive)*

6.　1　Becoming very good at something requires your being willing

　　_____
　　　　　　　　　　　　　(infinitive)

and _____ .
　　　　　　　　　　　(infinitive)

7.　Most of the letters were alike,

　　2　_____ and _____ .
　　　　　(present participle + infinitive)　　　　　*(infinitive)*

8. The small boy, / , stood alone on the corner,

    2/ _____
                                      (past participle)

    2 a tiny figure _____ .
                                       (infinitive)

9. 1 The old woman, / , sat in the overheated bus,

    2/ _____
                                        (past participle)

    2 _____ ,
                                        (past participle)

    2 and _____ .
                                        (past participle)

10. 1 She walked down the stairs,

    2 _____ but
                                        (present participle)

    2 _____ .
                                        (past participle – not a past tense verb)

EXERCISE C: reading for verb phrases   Accuracy _____

Directions: Now, read in a good book and find three sentences containing verb phrases used as modifiers, either bound or free, one each for the present participial, the past participial, and the infinitive phrase. Write out the sentences below, putting parentheses around each phrase. Also tell the title of the book and its author.

_____

_____

_____

_____

_____

_____

_____

_____

_____

Book title: _____

Author: _____

THE VERB PHRASE

EXERCISE D: using the verb phrase

Directions: In the following exercise, you are to use the given verb phrase in two different sentences, one as a bound modifier (without commas) and one as a free modifier (with commas). You may add modifiers to the phrase as you wish. Be careful not to use any of the phrases as main verbs or any of the *-ing* phrases as nouns (gerunds).

Example: *bounding along the busy street*

Bound modifier: The girl *bounding along the busy street with her load of newspapers* was running behind schedule.

Free modifier: He was on his way to buy a new mitt, *bounding along the busy street*, whistling happily.

1. *finding a better way*

   Bound modifier: _____
   _____

   Free modifier: _____
   _____

2. *stopped by a red light*

   Bound modifier: _____
   _____

   Free modifier: _____
   _____

3. *broken by the pounding surf*

   Bound modifier: _____
   _____

   Free modifier: _____
   _____

4. *to start again from the beginning*

   Bound modifier: _____
   _____

   Free modifier: _____
   _____

5. *hoping for the lead*

   Bound modifier: _____

   _____

   Free modifier: _____

   _____

6. *manufactured in South America*

   Bound modifier: _____

   _____

   Free modifier: _____

   _____

7. *to fulfill the requirement*

   Bound modifier: _____

   _____

   Free modifier: _____

   _____

8. *appearing before the court*

   Bound modifier: _____

   _____

   Free modifier: _____

   _____

9. *chosen by a committee of her peers*

   Bound modifier: _____

   _____

   Free modifier: _____

   _____

10. *arranged alphabetically*

   Bound modifier: _____

   _____

   Free modifier: _____

   _____

3. THE NOUN PHRASE

The next free modifier we will explore is the **noun phrase.** First, we will look at how to construct the phrase itself, using a variety of bound modifiers placed before the noun. Then we will go on to use the noun phrase thus created as a free modifier.

MODIFIERS THAT MAKE NOUN PHRASES

1.   **Descriptive adjectives, with adverbs and qualifiers:** It is, of course, common for a noun to be preceded by a descriptive adjective. In turn, that adjective may be accompanied by an adverb, and that adverb may be preceded by a special kind of adverb called a **qualifier.**

       (noun)   sunglasses
       (adjective + noun)   green sunglasses
       (adverb + adjective + noun)   dark green sunglasses
       (qualifier + adverb + adjective + noun)   very dark green sunglasses

The most common qualifiers are *very, quite, somewhat, rather, almost, fairly, nearly*, and *too*.

2.   **Limiting adjectives:** Limiting adjectives are words, other than the usual descriptive adjectives, that precede the noun and help to clarify, identify, or distinguish that noun from others.

       Articles—*a, an, the*
       Demonstratives—*this, that, these, those, a certain*
       Possessives—*my, your, his, her, its, our, their, whose, NOUN+ 's*
       Ordinals—*first, second, third...next, last*
       Quantifiers—*one, two, three...each, every, both, only, few, little, some, several,*
                                 many, most, all, any, another, no
       Comparatives and superlatives—*more, most, less, least, fewer, fewest*

Descriptive and limiting adjectives are the most simple of the noun modifiers. The remaining noun modifiers that we will examine are created by transforming them from some other role in the sentence.

3.   **Nouns as noun modifiers:**

       Original sentence: The breeze comes off the sea.
       Transformation: The *sea breeze* refreshed us as we walked home.

We know that *sea* in the noun phrase *the sea breeze* is not an adjective, because we cannot use it in any of the other adjective ways. We cannot say "The breeze was sea." Nor can we say "most sea" or "very sea." Other examples of nouns as modifiers would be *leather* coat, *mahogany* table, *water* bottle, and *office* furniture. Examples abound.

4.   **Participles as noun modifiers:**

The present participle

Original sentence: The leaves *fall* each October.
Transformation: The *falling* leaves swirl in the wind.

The present participial modifier may come from other parts of the original sentence.

Original sentence: The stick is used for *walking*.
Transformation: The *walking* stick stood by the back door.

The past participle

Original sentence: The record cold temperatures *froze* the lake.
First transformation: The lake was *frozen* by the record cold temperatures.
Final transformation: The *frozen* lake made a wonderful skating rink.

5.   **Two-part constructions as noun modifiers:**

The noun + present participle combination

Original sentence: The prisoner was *wielding* a *knife*.
Transformation: The *kinfe-wielding* prisoner was soon disarmed.

The noun + past participle combination

Original sentence: Fur *lines* my jacket.
First transformation: My jacket is *lined* with *fur*.
Final transformation: My *fur-lined* jacket kept me warm all winter.

The adjective + past participle combination

Original sentence: My sister pitches with her *left hand*.
Transformation: My *left-handed* sister led her team to the championship.

The adverb + past participle combination

Original sentence: The steak was *done* quite *well*.
Transformation: The *well-done* steak look delicious.

The adverb + present participle combination

Original sentence: The flames were *leaping high*.
Transformation: The *high-leaping* flames prevented the firemen from
                        entering the building.

Be aware of the punctuation issue in the adverb two-part constructions. If the adverb ends in *–ly*, there will be no hyphen between it and the participle.

Your *poorly written* paper will hurt your average this semester.

NOUN PHRASE AS FREE MODIFIER

All of the noun phrases we have constructed so far can be used in the primary noun functions of a sentence—as subject, direct object, indirect object, object of a preposition, or predicate noun. Let us now consider how the noun phrase may be used as a free modifier.

You are probably familiar with appositives, nouns placed alongside other nouns to provide a second way of expressing that person, place, thing, or idea. An appositive is one kind of noun phrase functioning as a free modifier. Look at this example, where the appositive, the Level 3/ set off by commas, is a free modifier.

> 2   Seated with Stuart and Brent Tarleton in the cool shade of the porch
>   of Tara, / , that bright April afternoon in 1861,
>   3/   her father's *plantation*
> 1   she made a pretty picture.
>   —Margaret Mitchell

There is always a complete correspondence between the appositive and the noun it is renaming—*Tara* and *plantation* are the same things, 100%. But other noun phrases offer only partial correspondence with the noun they are modifying. They serve more as subsets of the first noun, each offering one of several possible nouns that might be included in the original.

> 1   He could see everything about the man:
>   2   his sly cat's *smile*,
>   2   the *peak* of hair at the back of his head,
>   2   his hemispherical *stomach*,
>   2   his candy-striped *T-shirt*,
>   2   and his crepe-soled *shoes*.
>   —John Updike

In this sentence John Updike establishes a general image in the base clause using the pronoun *everything*. He then moves to specific elements of the character's appearance, using five different nouns as free modifiers. None of them singly corresponds to the word *everything*; in fact, the author could have named dozens of nouns and still not have covered everything that was to be seen. Instead, he has selected nouns that are distinctive and highly descriptive, helping to portray both the looks and the personality of his character.

Notice that the second free modifier, *peak*, is followed by descriptive prepositional phrases. Once the noun as free modifier has been established, it may itself have additional bound modifiers.

Here are other examples of sentences that have noun phrases as free modifiers.

> 1   The lighter's flame lighted up his features for an instant,
>   2   the packed rosy *jowl*,
>   2   the graying *temple* under Tyrolean hat's brim,
>   2   the bulging, blue, glazed *eye*.
>   —Kay Boyle

1   They will know nothing but the bleakest of New England scenery—
2   a few hard-bitten *pastures,*
2   a rocky *wall,*
2   a moth-eaten *hill* that is neither a bold mountain nor a stirring plain, and
2   a stern and paintless old *house.*   —D. C. Peattie

2   Sometimes when I am up in Maine and the men come to fix things—
   3   handsome, attractive people that they are,
      4   coming to fix a pipe, to measure, to take apart
         a motor, to drag a car to the garage—
1   often then I find myself falling into a flirtatiousness,
2   a sort of love for their *look,*
   3   their sunburned *faces,*
   3   their fine oiled *workshoes,*
   3   their *way* at the wheel of a truck,
   3   their *jokes* about the bill,
   3   their *ways* with other men,
      4   downtown drinking coffee, or
      4   inside a house under construction, or
      4   at the ravaged shed of the boatbuilder,
   3   their strong *fingers* yellowed from nicotine.
         —Elizabeth Hardwick

Note: In the last example, the word *look* was italicized in the original sentence, almost to suggest that the upcoming nouns are free modifiers describing that look.

Note also that *people* in the first Level 3 is an appositive to *men,* and in the second Level 2, *love* is an appositive to *flirtatiousness.*

THE NOUN PHRASE

Name:_____

EXERCISE A: noun modifiers

Accuracy _____ Creativity _____

Directions: Fill in the modifiers listed in the parentheses in order to complete the noun phrase. Work from right to left, backward from the noun of the second-level element. Refer back to the lesson to find suggestions that fit the categories. Draw on your own observation and experience for the words you use. The noun phrase will be an appositive to the noun printed in **bold** type.

1. 1   The teacher knew what to expect from the **boy** in the front row,

    2   the _____ , _____ _____
              (adjective)   *(adverb)*   *(adjective)*
         _____ clown.
                  (noun)

2. 1   Throughout grade school this **girl**, / , had been repeatedly elected to class office.

    2/ a/an _____ , _____ _____
                  (qualifier)   *(adverb)*   *(adjective)*
         _____ organizer.
         (adverb + past or present participle combination)

3. 1   By the age of eighteen his future **role** was well defined—

    2   the _____ _____ , _____
              (adverb)   *(adjective)*   *(noun + present participle combination)*

    rebel.

4. 1   The new school seemed to be a terrifying **place**,

    2   a/an _____ , _____ , _____ _____ building.
                (adjective)   *(adjective)*   *(qualifier)*   *(adjective)*

5. 1   The **road** stretched out for miles,

    2   a/an _____ , _____ _____ .
                (adjective)   *(past participle)*   *(noun)*

6. 1   Jennie had an uncanny **knack** for guessing the top ten songs of the week,

    2   a/an _____ , _____ skill.
                  (adjective)   *(adjective)*

7. 1   The toddler **giggled** at the antics of the monkey,

    2   a/an _____ , _____ ,
                    (past participle)   *(adverb + past participle combination)*

    _____ squeal.
            (adjective)

8. 1   Teddy was busily preparing the **main dish**,

    2   _____ _____ , _____
            (possessive)   *(adjective)*   *(noun + past participle combination)*
    chicken.

9. 1   Christine dreamed of being a great **explorer**,

    2   a/an _____ , _____ Columbus.
                    (adjective)   *(noun + present participle combination)*

10. 1   We hurried to join the playing **children**,

    2   a/an _____ , _____ , _____ trio.
                    (present participle)   *(present participle)*   *(adjective)*

EXERCISE B: reading for noun phrases   Accuracy _____

Directions: Now, read in a good book and find two sentences containing noun phrases as free modifiers. Write out the sentences below, putting parentheses around each phrase. Also tell the title of the book and its author.

_____

_____

_____

_____

_____

_____

_____

_____

_____

_____

Book title: _____

Author: _____

THE NOUN PHRASE

Name:_____

EXERCISE C: noun phrases

Accuracy _____ Creativity _____

Directions: These exercises will give you practice in extending the second-level elements to include more than one noun phrase.

1. 1   Peter found the **gifts** that he wanted most under the tree,

    2   _____ _____ _____ books and
        (quantifier)   (adjective)   (noun)

    2   _____ _____ , _____
        (article)   (adjective)   (noun + past participle combination)
        _____ jacket.
            (noun)

2. 1   Mother has thrown out all our **mess** —

    2   _____ _____ , _____ comics and
        (possessive)   (adjective)   (adjective)

    2   _____ _____ _____ , _____ models.
        (possessive)   (adverb)   (past participle)   (past participle)

3. 1   The **resources** of the library are limitless—

    2   _____ _____ reference books,
                (quantifier)   (noun)

    2   _____ _____ _____ first editions,
          (quantifier)   (adverb)   (past participle)

    2   _____ _____ _____ _____ collection, and
        (article)   (qualifier)   (adjective)   (noun)

    2   _____ _____ magazines and newspapers.
                (quantifier)   (adjective)

4. 1   They looked with dismay at the **yard** —

    2   _____ _____ , _____ hedges,
        (possessive)   (present participle)   (adjective)

    2   _____ _____ grass.
        (possessive)   (adverb + past participle combination)

5. 1   The platform was crowded with **luggage**:

    2   _____ _____ , _____ trunks and
         (quantifier)   (adverb)   (adjective)

    2   _____ _____ suitcases.
         (quantifier)   (noun + past participle combination)

In the remaining sentences you may write your own modifiers, using as many varieties as possible. Supply a word for each blank space. You may combine blanks to form compound constructions. Add commas as needed.

6.   1   It takes many **qualities** to make a good leader—

     2   _____ _____ _____ courage,

     2   _____ _____ _____ fear, and

     2   _____ _____ _____ patience,

7.   1   I'll never forget that last **summer** at camp—

     2   _____ _____ _____ days,

     2   _____ _____ _____ _____ evenings, and

     2   _____ _____ _____ _____

       _____ weeks.

8.   1   Kathy found that she liked **everything** about college—

     2   _____ _____ _____ courses,

     2   _____ _____ _____ dormitory, and

     2   _____ _____ _____ _____ dates.

9.   1   David carried in all the **packages** from the car—

     2   _____ _____ _____ groceries,

     2   _____ _____ shoes, and

     2   _____ _____ _____ presents.

10.   1   Sue drew a picture of her ideal **car**:

     2   _____ _____ _____ color,

     2   _____ _____ _____ trim, and

     2   _____ _____ _____ _____ wheels.

THE NOUN PHRASE

Name:_____

EXERCISE D: noun phrases

Accuracy _____ Creativity _____

Directions: In this exercise, you have been given base clauses containing nouns printed in **bold** type, along with spaces to fill in noun phrases as free modifiers. Try to use a variety of modifiers before your noun, then add bound modifiers after the noun if you wish.

1. 1 We held our secret meetings in a **place** no one would find us,

    2 _____

        _____ .

2. 1 Sara and Phil spared no expense on the **decorations** —

    2 _____

        _____ ,

    2 _____

        _____ ,

    2 _____

        _____ .

3. 1 The governor assembled a truly diverse **committee** to study the issue:

    2 _____

        _____ ,

    2 _____

        _____ ,

    2 _____

        _____ .

4. 1 **Nobody** could persuate him to reconsider,

    2 not _____

    _____ ,

    2 not _____

    _____ ,

    2 not even _____

    _____ .

5. 1 We had only two **alternatives**,

    2 _____

    _____ , or

    2 _____

    _____ .

6. 1 I finally found **what** I had been looking for,

    2 _____

    _____ .

7. 1 **Cheryl Higginbottom**, / , is coming to dinner tonight.

    2/ _____

    _____

8. 1 Suddenly he was caught between his two worst **enemies,**

    2 _____

    _____ , and

    2 _____

    _____ .

9. 1 She was in charge of the petting zoo **animals**,

    2 _____

       _____ ,

    2 _____

       _____ , and

    2 _____

       _____ .

10. 1 It was a pleasure to meet your **relatives**,

    2 both_____

       _____ ,

    2 and _____

       _____ .

4. THE ABSOLUTE PHRASE

The absolute phrase, while rarely heard in everyday conversation, is a common characteristic of mature writing. In keeping with the principles of addition and levels of generality we discussed in Chapter 1, the absolute phrase enables the writer to present a complete action in the base clause and then add selected details, which allow the reader to experience the action in smaller, more specific units.

An absolute phrase is derived from a sentence that contains the verb *was* or *were* either as a helping verb or as the complete verb. Removing *was* or *were* from the sentence leaves us with two parts, called the subject and the predicate of the absolute phrase.

Just as there are many grammatical constructions that may follow *was* or *were*, so there are many varieties of predicate for the absolute phrase. Let's now look at the kinds of predicates found in absolute phrases and how they are formed.

1. **Present participle used as absolute predicate:**

Main clause:	We walked on.
Sentence to be added:	The crust was cracking uneasily under us.
Remove *was* or *were* :	*was*
Resulting absolute phrase:	the crust cracking uneasily under us
Final sentence:	

   > 1 We walked on,
   >   2 the crust *cracking* uneasily under us.   —John Knowles

2. **Past participle used as absolute predicate:**

Main clause:	Apple trees bloomed in the dusk.
Sentence to be added:	The last of daylight was seemingly sucked up into their white petals.
Remove *was* or *were* :	*was*
Resulting absolute phrase:	the last of daylight seemingly sucked up into their white petals
Final sentence:	

   > 1 Apple trees bloomed in the dusk,
   >   2 the last of daylight seemingly *sucked* up into their white petals.
   >   —Jessamyn West

Note: Be careful here that you do not write a run-on sentence, that is, two or more independent clauses joined only by commas. A phrase such as *her eyes closed* could be either an independent clause, using the past tense verb *closed*, or an absolute phrase using the past participle, which is also *closed*. You usually can make sure that you have an absolute phrase by reinserting *was* or *were*. Here is an example in which *her eyes closed* is clearly an absolute phrase.

> 1 She sat quietly in the back seat of the car,
> 2 her eyes closed and
> 2 her hands folded in her lap.

Each Level 2 modifier is based on a sentence: her eyes *were* closed and her hands *were* folded.

3. Infinitive used as absolute predicate:

Main clause:	About one-third of these will leave high school without graduating.
Sentences to be added:	The boys were to enter the army or the labor market.
	The girls were to enter the labor market or to marry without entering it.
Remove *was* or *were* :	*were*
Resulting absolute phrases:	the boys to enter the army or the labor market
	the girls to enter the labor market or to marry without entering it

Final sentence:

> 1 About one-third of these will leave high school without graduating,
> 2 the boys *to enter* the army or the labor market,
> 2 the girls *to enter* the labor market or *to marry* without entering it.
>   —Reuel Denney

4. Noun used as absolute predicate:

Main clause:	He dressed slowly.
Sentence to be added:	The softness of his shirt...was a reward against his skin....
Remove *was* or *were* :	*was*
Resulting absolute phrase:	the softness of his shirt...a reward against his skin...

Final sentence:

> 1 He dressed slowly,
> 2 the softness of his shirt ...a *reward* against his skin....—Irwin Shaw

5. **Pronoun used as absolute predicate:**

Main clause:	They ate in silence.
Sentence to be added:	The only sound was that of the clicking knives and sweeping spoons.
Remove *was* or *were* :	*was*
Resulting absolute phrase:	the only sound that of the clicking knives and sweeping spoons

Final sentence:

1 They ate in silence,
    2 the only sound *that* of the clicking knives and sweeping spoons.
                    —E. M. Roberts

Common pronouns that can become absolute predicates include *this, that, these, those, some, any, none, all, most, everything, nothing, something.*

6. **Adjective used as absolute predicate:**

Main clause:	The hunter moved his shoulder under the weight of the ducks.
Sentence to be added:	His mind was full for the moment with the image of his father's face....
Remove *was* or *were* :	*was*
Resulting absolute phrase:	his mind full for the moment with the image of his father's face...

Final sentence:

1 The hunter moved his shoulder under the weight of the ducks,
    2 his mind *full* for the moment with the image of his father's face....
                    —Wallace Stegner

7. **Adverb used as absolute predicate:**

Main clause:	A porter came out from under the shelter of the station.
Sentence to be added:	His shoulders were up against the rain.
Remove *was* or *were* :	*was*
Resulting absolute phrase:	his shoulders up against the rain

Final sentence:

1 A porter came out from under the shelter of the station,
    2 his shoulders *up* against the rain. —Ernest Hemingway

8. **Prepositional phrase used as absolute predicate:**

Main clause:	She bought a pack of cigarettes from Luke and went out again.
Sentence to be added:	A handkerchief was around her head....
Remove *was* or *were* :	*was*
Resulting absolute phrase:	a handkerchief around her head...

Final sentence:
    1 She bought a pack of cigarettes from Luke and went out again,
        2 a handkerchief *around her head* ....—John Updike

One preposition in particular, *like*, may be used to create a predicate for the absolute phrase that is offering a **comparison**.

Main clause:	He slowly turns.
Sentence to be added:	His eyes were like those of a dead fish.
Remove *was* or *were* :	*were*
Resulting absolute phrase:	his eyes like those of a dead fish
Final sentence:	

    1 He slowly turns,
        2 his eyes *like those of a dead fish.* —Eugene O'Neill

Preposition *with* as the marker of the absolute phrase: Sometimes an absolute phrase will begin with the word *with*, called the "marker" of the absolute. It is especially useful to indicate that what is being written is indeed an absolute phrase and not a run-on sentence. Here is a sentence you saw earlier; it is much clearer when the marker *with* introduces the absolute phrase.

    1 She sat quietly in the back seat of the car,
        2 *with* her eyes closed and
        2 her hands folded in her lap.

The marker *with* might also help the sentence read more smoothly or add a touch of style.

Main clause:	In the wagon box behind was Ina's white pine coffin.
Sentence to be added:	Frost was on the heads of the nails.
Remove *was* or *were* :	*were*
Resulting absolute phrase:	frost on the heads of the nails
Add the marker *with* :	with frost on the heads of the nails

        Final sentence:
            1 In the wagon box behind was Ina's white pine coffin,
                2 *with* frost on the heads of the nails.—Wallace Stegner

Compound subjects and predicates of the absolute: Both the subject and the predicate can be compounded in the absolute phrase. Look at the following examples.

1   He dressed slowly,
  2   *the softness of his shirt and the soft warmth of his wool socks and his flannel trousers* a reward against his skin after the harsh pressure of the shoulder harness and thigh and hip pads.
     —Irwin Shaw

1   She nodded several times,
  2   her hair *swaying with the wide, circular movements of her head, then hanging still as she kept her head bowed to him.*
     —Ayn Rand

The list below summarizes the nine possible predicates of the absolute that we have covered; all are using the same subject, *his sport coat*. Imagine what the Level 1 base clause might be for each of these absolute phrases.

his sport coat (was)

ripping at the shoulders	**Present participle**
wrinkled from lying on the floor of his closet	**Past participle**
to be sent to the cleaners	**Infinitive**
a wonderful bargain from the school rummage sale	**Noun**
one of those with the wide lapels	**Pronoun**
old but still fashionable	**Adjective**
down to his knees	**Adverb**
on a hook by the back door	**Prepositional phrase**
like a Houdini straitjacket	**Comparison**

How many of the above absolute phrases could be introduced with the marker *with*?

THE ABSOLUTE PHRASE

Name:_____

EXERCISE A: writing absolute phrases

Accuracy _____ Creativity _____

Directions: This set of exercises will emphasize the variety of predicates the absolute phrase may have. Provide the type of absolute predicate called for, then feel free to attach additional elements to the predicate as you wish.

Example: 1   He watched the tennis match,
                   2   his head *swiveling.*
                              or
                   2   his head *swiveling as the action speeded up.*

1. 1   She erased the blackboard carefully,

    2   the eraser _____ .
                         (present participle as predicate)

2. 1   He stepped out into the bright sunlight,

    2   his eyes _____ .
                         (past participle as predicate)

3. 1   They arrived at the fairground early,

    2   the adults _____ ,
                         (infinitive as predicate)
    2   the children _____ .
                         (infinitive as predicate)

4. 1   Well-planned landscaping changed the whole atmosphere of the little park,

    2   carefully braced saplings _____ .
                         (noun as predicate)

5. 1   They cooked for themselves while their parents were out of town,

    2   their meals _____ .
                         (indefinite pronoun as predicate)

6. 1   A noisy, wiggly troop erupted from the school bus when it stopped at the zoo,

    2   happy children _____ .
                         (adjective as predicate)

7. 1   The gymnastics coach demonstrated the beginning position of the exercise,

    2   her arms _____ .
             (adverb as predicate)

8. 1   The young soldier settled himself in the train seat a bit self-consciously,

    2   an elaborately wrapped pink box _____ .
             (prepositional phrase as predicate)

9. 1   She played her graduation recital with great enthusiasm,

    2   her hands _____ .
             (comparison as predicate)

10. 1   The orchestra assembled on the vast stage,

    2   with _____ .
         (with as a marker of the absolute; add a noun and any kind of predicate)

THE ABSOLUTE PHRASE

Name:_____

EXERCISE B: combining sentences

Accuracy_____

Directions: For each of the following sets of sentences, use the first sentence as your base clause. Then develop one or more absolute phrases, incorporating the information given in the remaining sentences.

1. The desk was arranged for a busy day's work. There was an array of newly sharpened pencils. They were in a painted mug. There were piles of paper and file cards within easy reach.

    1 _____

       2 _____

       2 _____

2. August's sizzling winds burned the buildings. Roofs were buckling from the heat. Walls were hot to the touch.

    1 _____

       2 _____

       2 _____

3. She held the tablecloth carefully. It was delicate handmade lace. It was spread over her outstretched fingers.

    1 _____

       2 _____

4. He presided ceremoniously over the barbecue. The concoctions were his own. The results were something best left undescribed.

    1 _____

       2 _____

       2 _____

5. They were paralyzed by the flood. Damage reports were still coming in. The death toll was still rising.

    1 _____

       2 _____

       2 _____

6. For various reasons they were eager to get to the beach. Some of them were eager to swim. Some were eager to play volleyball. Others were just eager to explore the tidal pools.

    1 _____

       2 _____

       2 _____

       2 _____

7. The first performance of the hit movie was sold out. Ticket-holders were waiting restlessly in the lobby for the second showing. The ushers were trying to keep them in a line.

    1 _____

       2 _____

       2 _____

8. They came home from the fishing trip disgusted. Their clothes were soaked. Their hands were empty.

    1 _____

       2 _____

       2 _____

9. The campus center filled a need. The students were using it daily as a combination study lounge and fast-food emporium.

    1 _____

       2 _____

10. The family had scattered for the day's vacation. The boys were hiking up in the mountains. The girls were biking over to a friend's house. Their parents were sailing out on the lake.

    1 _____

       2 _____

       2 _____

       2 _____

THE ABSOLUTE PHRASE

Name:_____

EXERCISE C: writing with absolute phrases

Accuracy _____ Creativity _____

Directions: These sentences will give you more opportunity to develop your own absolute phrases. Try to use as wide a variety of predicates as you can. Remember that you are free to add other elements to the predicate wherever they are appropriate. Supply your own commas and periods.

1. 1   The audience was caught up in the mood of the play,

    2   their laughter _____ and

    _____ .

2. 1   The patient waiting for X-rays sat in the stuffy reception room,

    2   her face _____ and

    _____ .

3. 1   Paintings lined the walls at the art exhibition,

    2   their colors _____ ,

    2   their subjects _____ .

4. 1   The president's speech lay ready on the desk,

    2   bound copies _____

    _____ .

5. 1   He was a familiar figure on the campus,

    2   his habitual costume _____ and

    _____ .

6. 1   They arrived at the cottage heavily laden,

    2   their diving equipment and their clothes _____

    _____ .

7. 1   The traffic was snarled at the intersection,

    2   the cars _____ .

8. 1   Everyone was seated for Grandpa's birthday celebration,

    2   with _____

    _____ .

9. 1   They finally managed to clean out the attic,

    2   the usable children's toys _____ ,

    2   the empty trunks _____ .

10. 1   The yard sale was a great success,

    2   many of the silliest knickknacks_____ ,

    2   some of the big-ticket items_____ .

EXERCISE D: reading for absolute phrases   Accuracy _____

Directions: Now, read in a good book and find two sentences containing absolute phrases. Write out the sentences below, putting parentheses around each absolute phrase. Also tell the title of the book and its author.

    Hint: Absolute phrases are most easily found in fiction, where there is action going on. Also, they are rarely found in dialogue, as people generally just don't talk that way.

_____

_____

_____

_____

_____

_____

Book title: _____

Author: _____

5. THE ADJECTIVE CLAUSE

A clause is a group of related words that contains a subject and a verb. If the clause expresses a complete thought and is able to stand by itself, we call it an **independent clause**. If the clause does not express a complete thought and is therefore unable to stand by itself, we call it a **dependent clause** or, sometimes, a **subordinate clause**.

There are three kinds of dependent clauses: the **noun clause**, the **adjective clause**, and the **adverb clause**. The noun clause usually does not act as a modifier but instead serves in the usual noun functions in a sentence. Here are a few examples of sentences containing noun clauses. The noun clauses are printed in italics.

(subject)	*That they had found the treasure* seemed doubtful.
(direct object)	The police didn't know *whether the shopkeeper was telling the truth*.
(object of preposition)	Your paper had nothing to do with *what I asked you to write about*.
(predicate nominative)	The best part was *that we were able to go on all the rides for free*.

In this book we will be most interested in the adjective and adverb clauses, because they serve as modifiers and may be either bound or free.

The adjective clause is a dependent clause that describes a noun or a pronoun. It is a useful way to combine two sentences that have a noun or pronoun in common, avoiding repetition. We will call one of those sentences the *receiver* sentence and the other the *donor* sentence. In the examples that follow in this chapter, the receiver sentence does not change at all. The donor sentence, however, will drop the repeated noun or pronoun and replace it with a **relative pronoun** or **relative adverb**. The adjective clause thus created (sometimes called a relative clause) will then be placed as closely as possible after the noun or pronoun it is modifying.

RELATIVE PRONOUNS

Here are several common relative pronouns:

who	whose	whom	which	that
whoever	whosever	whomever	whichever	

The relative pronouns *who, whose,* and *whom* replace a human noun or pronoun; *which* replaces a nonhuman noun or pronoun; *that* replaces either a human or nonhuman noun or pronoun. In some of the examples you will see in the next few pages, the adjective clause has been written as a bound, or restrictive, modifier, not set off from the word it is modifying by any punctuation. As was true with restrictive verb phrases, a **restrictive adjective clause** is necessary to define, or restrict, the noun or pronoun we are talking about.

In other examples, the adjective clause has been written as a free modifier, a **nonrestrictive adjective clause**, set off from the main clause by a comma. It is providing useful information at a lower level of generality, but it could be removed without leaving the reader in doubt about the identity of the modified noun or pronoun. Always be aware of the difference in meaning when you change the punctuation.

An adjective clause as a bound modifier modifying a nonhuman noun or pronoun may begin with either *which* or *that*, although some people prefer to use only *that* for such a clause. An adjective clause as a free modifier, however, will almost always begin with *which*.

1. **Relative pronoun used to replace the subject:**

Receiver sentence:	The children moved away.
Donor sentence:	*The children* sang so beautifully.
Relative pronoun:	*who*
Final sentence:	The children *who sang so beautifully* moved away.

Receiver sentence:	I gave away the bicycle.
Donor sentence:	*The bicycle* had a bent frame.
Relative pronoun:	*that* (or *which*)
Final sentence:	I gave away the bicycle *that* (or *which*) *had a bent frame.*

2. **Relative pronoun used to replace a possessive noun or pronoun:**

Receiver sentence:	The mother stayed overnight at the hospital.
Donor sentence:	*Her boy* was operated on.
Relative pronoun:	*whose*
Final sentence:	The mother *whose boy was operated on* stayed overnight at the hospital.

3. **Relative pronoun used to replace the direct object:** If the relative pronoun is not already at the beginning of the adjective clause, it must be moved into that position when it is replacing a direct object. In these examples, pay attention to that shift.

Receiver sentence:	The worker received a promotion.
Donor sentence:	Ms. Brooks recommended *the worker.*
Relative pronoun:	*whom*
Final sentence:	The worker *whom Ms. Brooks recommended* received a promotion.

Receiver sentence:	The check took care of all expenses.
Donor sentence:	She enclosed *the check.*
Relative pronoun:	*that* (or *which*)
Final sentence:	The check *that* (or *which*) *she enclosed* took care of all expenses.

Receiver sentence:	The car was in the medium price range.
Donor sentence:	He bought *a car.*
Relative pronoun:	*that* (or *which*)
Final sentence:	The car *that* (or *which*) *he bought* was in the medium price range.

4. **Relative pronouns used as replacements in prepositional phrases:** When a relative pronoun is replacing an object of the preposition in formal writing, both the preposition and the relative pronoun will move to the beginning of the clause.

Receiver sentence:	Mr. Smith felt cheated.
Donor sentence:	She sold the car to *Mr. Smith*.
Relative pronoun:	*whom*
Final sentence:	Mr. Smith, *to whom she sold the car*, felt cheated.

Receiver sentence:	Mr. Jones threatened legal action.
Donor sentence:	The check was written on *Mr. Jones's* account.
Relative pronoun:	*whose*
Final sentence:	Mr. Jones, *on whose account the check was written*, threatened legal action.

Receiver sentence:	The house was in need of major repairs.
Donor sentence:	He lived in *the house*.
Relative pronoun:	*which*
Final sentence:	The house *in which he lived* was in need of major repairs.

The relative pronoun *that* is not interchangeable with *which* in a prepositional phrase. You could not write *The house in that he lived was in need of major repairs*. You could, however, write *The house that he lived in was in need of major repairs*.

5. **Omitted relative pronoun:** When the relative pronoun replaces either the direct object or the object of a preposition, the pronoun can often be omitted. Of the previous examples, several could change.

> The worker *Ms. Brooks recommended* received a promotion.
> The check *she enclosed* took care of all expenses.
> The car *he bought* was in the medium price range.
> The house *he lived in* was in need of major repairs.

6. **Relative pronoun *which* used to replace the entire donor sentence:** In some cases the relative pronoun *which* may refer to the entire idea expressed by the donor sentence.

> The two kids that I had seen before left early, *which seemed very strange to me*.
> —James Herbert

Receiver sentence:	The two kids that I had seen before left early.
Donor sentence:	[*The fact that the two kids I had seen before left early*] seemed very strange to me.
Relative pronoun:	*which*
Final sentence:	The two kids that I had seen before left early, *which seemed very strange to me*.

RELATIVE ADVERBS

Sometimes an author will write a sentence that contains a noun of place or time. This might then be followed by a sentence containing the same noun as the object of a preposition. In such a case, writers will often join the sentences by substituting the relative adverb *where* or *when* for the entire prepositional phrase, rather than use the more formal *in which* or *on which*.

1. **Relative adverb *where* used to modify a noun expressing place:**

   ...they went into the chilly, bare little entry, *where overshoes and a fibre mat were piled*.
   —Ruth Suckow

Receiver sentence:	...they went into the chilly, bare little entry.
Donor sentence:	Overshoes and a fibre mat were piled *in the chilly, bare little entry*.
Relative adverb:	*where* [*in which*]
Final sentence:	...they went into the chilly, bare little entry, *where overshoes and a fibre mat were piled*.

2. **Relative adverb *when* used to modify a noun expressing time:**

   He sometimes thought of those mornings when she used to get up before daylight to go duckshooting with him on the river: the heavy silence over the dew-drenched fields, the dark sound of the waters, the quick flush of dawn in the east and the waking of the breeze in the tops of the cottonwoods, the birds singing in the pearl-coloured air.
   —Willa Cather

Receiver sentence:	He sometimes thought of those mornings.
Donor sentence:	On *those mornings* she used to get up before daylight....
Relative adverb:	*when* [*on which*]
Final sentence:	He sometimes thought of those mornings *when she used to get up before daylight ....*

THE ADJECTIVE CLAUSE

Name:_____

EXERCISE A: combining sentences

Accuracy_____

Directions: In these exercises, you are to combine the donor sentence with the receiver sentence by changing the donor sentence into an adjective clause, as either a free or a bound modifier. Keep in mind that there is a difference in the way free and bound modifiers are punctuated.

Example: Receiver sentence: The man was frowning in concentration.
              Donor sentence: The man sat beside me.
              Final sentence: The man who sat beside me was frowning
                               in concentration.

1.   Receiver sentence: The lifeguard wished she had an umbrella over her rowboat.
     Donor sentence: The lifeguard's nose was beginning to peel.

   _____

   _____

2.   Receiver sentence: The wrecking ball crashed against the wall of the stately old house.
     Donor sentence: The stately old house had been a famous landmark.

   _____

   _____

3.   Receiver sentence: The grass grew ankle-deep in the corner of the park.
     Donor sentence: In the corner of the park there was a hidden spring.

   _____

   _____

4.   Receiver sentence: She was afraid that she would not have enough vanilla for the recipe.
     Donor sentence: She had chosen the recipe.

   _____

   _____

5.   Receiver sentence: The boy was unable to go at the last moment.
     Donor sentence: The class had elected the boy as a delegate to the conference.

   _____

   _____

6. Receiver sentence: The group marched smartly behind the parade marshal.
   Donor sentence: The group was carrying the colors.

   _____

   _____

7. Receiver sentence: The lightning blew out all our fuses.
   Donor sentence: The lightning struck our metal flagpole.

   _____

   _____

8. Receiver sentence: The masks were displayed in the main library.
   Donor sentence: The students had made masks for the play.

   _____

   _____

9. Receiver sentence: Give this delivery to Joan or Bill.
   Donor sentence: One arrives first.

   _____

   _____

10. Receiver sentence: Someone may be able to give us directions.
    Donor sentence: Someone is coming out of the building now.

   _____

   _____

Note: Look back over your answers. In three of them, you could have omitted the relative pronoun. Which ones?

   # _____   # _____   # _____

THE ADJECTIVE CLAUSE

Name:_____

EXERCISE B: writing adjective clauses

Accuracy _____ Creativity _____

Directions: For each of the following sentences you are to supply adjective clauses, either bound or free, that modify the words in **bold type**. The last two sentences have additional directions.

1. 1   The **seniors**, / , waited for the final bell.

    2/ _____

2. 1   The **car** _____ had bad **brakes**,

    2   _____ .

3. 1   She bought a large **print** by Picasso,

    2   _____ .

4. 1   Those bright **searchlights**, / , made her wonder about the **person** _____

    _____ .

    2/ _____

5. 1   Invite **anyone** _____ ,

    2   perhaps **someone** _____ .

6. 1   From the hilltop they looked down the winding **road**,

    2   _____ .

7. 1   The **book** of Spanish poems, / , lay **on top of the radio**,

    2/ _____

    2   _____

8. 1   **Everything** _____

    was happening in the **kitchen**,

    2   _____ .

9. 1   They bought the first **house** _____ ,

    2   _____ .
        (refer broadly the act of buying the house, not just to the house itself)

10. 1   The **project** _____ reached a point

        _____ ,

    2   _____ .
        (comment on the entire Level 1)

EXERCISE C: reading for adjective clauses   Accuracy_____

Directions: Now, read in a good book and find three sentences containing adjective clauses. Write out the sentences below, putting parentheses around each adjective clause.

   Also tell the title of the book and its author.

_____

_____

_____

_____

_____

_____

_____

_____

_____

_____

Book title: _____

Author: _____

6. THE ADVERB CLAUSE

The adverb clause is another type of dependent clause that may be used as a bound or free modifier. Like a simple adverb, the adverb clause will usually answer such questions as *when?, where?, how?, why?, how much?,* or *under what conditions?.*

To create an adverb clause, you will use a subordinating conjunction. This is a word (or two or three) that allows an independent clause to be joined to another sentence or sentence part. Here are the subordinating conjunctions that help create adverb clauses.

after	although	as	because	before	if
lest	once	since	than	though	till
unless	until	when (ever)	where (ever)	whereas	while
as if	as soon as	as though	even if	even though	
in case	in order that	provided that	so that		

The following examples show how a subordinating conjunction may be added to a sentence to form an adverb clause.

although	+	we will have to be back before dinner
because	+	the tomatoes were on sale this week
in case	+	they get caught in the rain

The subordinate clause thus constructed may then serve as either a bound or a free modifier.

Adverb clause as bound modifier in the base clause:

> 1   The sense of being crowded by ghosts was even more real *because there was practically no furniture in the house.*
> —Horace Sutton

The adverb clause here is modifying the phrase *was even more real*, telling why.

Adverb clause as bound modifier in lower level:

> 1   I saw Miss Pettigrew again at Mass next morning,
> 2   kneeling a little in front of me,
> 2   resting her head upon her missal *as if she could not bear the weight of head on neck.*
> —Muriel Spark

The adverb clause here is modifying the phrase *resting her head upon her missal*, telling how.

As a free modifier, the adverb clause usually modifies the entire sentence, rather than a single word or phrase; it works at a lower level of generality to bring the entire action of the sentence into sharper focus.

Adverb clause as a free modifier:

> 2 *And when they asked for money,*
> > 3 Bhuaji or the other relatives,

1 as often as not she gave—
> 2 quite absentmindedly,
> 2 taking out her keys to unlock the steel almira in which she kept her cashbox,
> > 3 *while they eagerly, greedily, watched her.*

—Ruth Prawler Jhabvala

THE ADVERB CLAUSE

Name:_____

EXERCISE A: writing adverb clauses

Accuracy _____ Creativity _____

Directions: Complete the following sentences by inserting adverb clauses where indicated, as either bound or free modifiers.

1. 1 She left the room _____

_____ ,

    2 grateful for a chance to stretch her legs.

2. 1 He hurried along the street,

    2 intent on reaching home _____

_____ ,

    3 _____ .

3. 1 The attorney punched both the "Up" and "Down" call buttons for the elevator,

    2 _____ .

4. 1 The gardener leaned on her shovel _____

_____ ,

    2 her eyes bright _____

_____ .

5. 1 The old cabinetmaker paused in his work,

    2 somewhat discouraged _____

_____ ,

    3 _____ .

(please note that this adverb clause goes with sentence #5)

6. 2 _____ ,

    1 people dashed into the supermarket through the rain,

    2 _____ .

7. 1   The butterfly rested on the leaf, immobile,

    2   _____

    _____ .

8. 1   Police cars closed in from all directions _____

    _____ ,

    2   their sirens screaming _____ .

9. 1   Few people remembered the little town—

    2   _____

    _____ .

10. 1   They stood looking at their hasty repair job _____

    _____ ,

    2   a minor miracle,

    3   _____

    _____ .

EXERCISE B: reading for adverb clauses   Accuracy_____

Directions: Now, read in a good book and find three sentences containing adverb clauses. Write out the sentences below, putting parentheses around each adverb clause.
    Also tell the title of the book and its author.

_____

_____

_____

_____

_____

_____

Book title: _____

Author: _____

THE ADVERB CLAUSE

Name:_____

EXERCISE C: writing adverb clauses

Accuracy _____ Creativity _____

Directions: The following exercises give you an opportunity to supply most of the material for your sentences. You must use at least one, but not more than two, adverb clauses with each base clause. They may be bound or free. You may add other modifiers if you choose.

The possible arrangements of the base clause and the adverb clauses are numerous. Here are a few possibilities, as reminders. The adverb clauses are in italics.

Examples: He decided to see the world. (base clause)

He decided to see the world *when he left the Army, since he had never been overseas.*

Even though he did not have much money, he finally decided to see the world, *because he was not yet ready to settle down.*

Whatever the consequences might be, he decided to see the whole wide world *as soon as he finished school.*

1. The moon rose.

_____

_____

_____

2. Rows of cans filled the shelves.

_____

_____

_____

3. She closed the door behind her.

_____

_____

_____

4. The drone hummed above them.

_____

_____

_____

5. A strange noise filled the air.

_____

_____

_____

6. Grandmother's glasses kept slipping down her nose.

_____

_____

_____

7. The pony stood trembling beside the fence.

_____

_____

_____

8. The question was settled.

_____

_____

_____

9. She waited patiently.

_____

_____

_____

10. They counted the money.

_____

_____

_____

7. NARRATION

Up to this point you have been studying the building blocks of good writing, the bound and free modifiers. You have seen how those modifiers, when used with the principles of **addition** and **levels of generality**, allow you to write a wide variety of sentence structures with confidence and ease.

The remainder of this book will show you different ways to apply these techniques to varied writing situations. In the next three chapters we will look at the topics of narration, description, and exposition; then, we will finish with a close examination of that larger unit of writing, the paragraph. As we progress from creative writing to essay writing, from fiction to nonfiction, you will see that the same guiding principles you have studied so far will continue to apply.

SHARPENING THE IMAGE PROPOSED BY THE VERB

When we speak of narration, we mean that part of a story concerned with the action, from Snape breathing down their necks, to an angry mob of French peasants storming the Bastille. The part of the sentence that expresses the action is the verb. In this chapter we will discuss the techniques that good writers use to bring their verbs to life.

There are three methods of sharpening the image proposed by the verb: adding detail, indicating quality, and making a comparison. The following sentence shows all three methods in use.

1	The gypsy was walking out toward the bull again,		
	2	walking heel-and-toe,	**Detail**
		3 insultingly,	**Quality**
		3 like a ballroom dancer	**Comparison**
		3 the red shafts of the banderillos twitching with his walk.	**Detail**

—Ernest Hemingway

Detail

By presenting the general action in the base clause, then moving to lower levels of generality to point out specific details, an author brings the reader closer to the action. Hemingway metaphorically brings binoculars to our eyes as we "zoom in" on the feet of the gypsy and the shafts of the banderillos.

In narrative writing, the detail itself will be a noun. It usually will appear within a present participial phrase, or it will serve as the subject of an absolute phrase whose predicate begins with a present participle. It is that noun/present participle combination that allows us to show the action of the base clause more clearly.

Quality

By quality in narrative writing we mean the ordinary adverb of manner, one that tells how the action is taking place. The walk of the gypsy had the quality of insult or arrogance about it.

While adverbs of time or place are common in good narrative writing, adverbs of manner are relatively rare. They tend to be abstract or too general, or they are merely shortcuts, showing the reaction of the observer to the action rather than picturing the action itself. Therefore, in this chapter, there will be no exercises using this method to sharpen the verb.

Comparison

A comparison in narrative writing depicts how one action is being performed by showing its similarities to another, familiar activity. The most common method used to express a comparison is a prepositional phrase beginning with *like*. Variations such as *hawklike* or *childishly*, or a present participle such as *snaking*, or an adverb clause beginning with *as if* or *as though* are also useful constructions to make comparisons.

NARRATIVE DETAILS USING PRESENT PARTICIPIAL PHRASES

A present participial phrase as a free modifier is the first method of presenting narrative details that we will explore. We have divided the details themselves into three categories: visual, nonvisual, and special.

Visual details

A visual detail is a smaller element of the action, something we would see better if we stood closer, such as a physical part of the performer of the action or a smaller part of the noun being acted upon in the base clause.

Here are some sentences demonstrating the use of present participial phrases to picture visual details.

> 1   He grinned confidingly and sank down on my cot,
>   2   leaning on his elbow in a relaxed, at-home way. —John Knowles

> 1   "Bye," said the car-hop,
>   2   opening a heart-shaped pocket over her heart and
>   2   dropping the tip courteously within.
>   —Eudora Welty

>   2   On the high rocks above,
> 1   egrets were balancing on one long slender leg,
>   2   raising the other in various balletic postures.
> 1   Others were flying,
>   2   fanning their gorgeous snow-white wings with panache.
>   —Jung Chang

Nonvisual details

Besides the information provided by our eyes, we have four other senses to help us experience an action—hearing, smell, taste, and touch. The sound of the baseball as it strikes the catcher's mitt, the aroma of crayons in the kindergarten classroom, the saliva-inducing flavor of a tomato fresh from the garden, the feel of the cool earth as we plant a tulip bulb—all of these details help make the moment unique and memorable for your reader.

In the next three sentences, the authors have used present participial phrases to make more vivid the action that was presented in a general way in the base clause.

>   2   Bumping across the car tracks,
>   2   easing the car over the rutted intersection,
>   2   feeling the built-up springs sink heavily, clear down, on a slow bump,
> 1   he swung left to avoid the main street.
>   —Wallace Stegner

> 1   His father left,
> 2   trailing the faint, unfamiliar, prosperous aroma of his cigar.
>
> —John Knowles

> 1   The rock had the comfort of spareness,
> 2   resisting the spine firmly,
> 3   like lying on the floor.   —Nadine Gordimer

Special details

The last type of narrative detail is called special because it conveys the action in a way that goes beyond just the senses. A special detail may express a delicate observation, a subtle hint of character or mood, or an imaginative rendering of an experience.

If you and your friends were enjoying the same activity—an afternoon at the beach, for example—all of you would see the water, hear the waves, feel the warmth of the sun on the back of your neck, smell the suntan lotion, and taste the lemonade from the cooler. These are visual and nonvisual details that all of you might mention if you were to write about that day.

Special details, however, are unique to each writer. For example, only you might compare the screams of the seagulls to Poseidon's hiccups, or pretend to be an explorer first setting foot on that shore, or remember the day your grandfather taught you how to build a real sandcastle. These details elevate the writing from the merely observable, into the realms of imagination, creativity, emotion, memory, desire, and personality.

Here are two sentences using present participial phrases to convey special details.

> 1   He enunciated daintily,
> 2   pushing the words away from him with his tongue.
>
> —Hortense Calisher

> 1   An owl went by,
> 2   extinguishing sound,
> 2   absorbing the soft trill of cricket and locust in its soft feathers.
>
> —Jessamyn West

NARRATION

Name:_____

EXERCISE A: details in present participial phrases

Accuracy _____ Creativity _____

Directions: In the following sentences, fill in each blank with a present participial phrase that provides either a visual detail, a nonvisual detail, or a special detail, as indicated.

1. 1   The boys ran to the playground,

  2   _____

   (visual detail)

   _____ ,

  2   _____

   (nonvisual detail)

   _____ .

2. 1   The child played with the dolls,

  2   _____

   (nonvisual detail)

   _____ ,

  2   _____

   (special detail)

   _____ .

3. 1   She gazed blankly at the test,

  2   _____

   (visual detail)

   _____ .

4. 1   Her mother moved quickly about the house,

  2   _____

   (visual detail)

   _____ ,

  2   _____

   (visual detail)

   _____ .

5. 1   He struggled with the locked door,

    2   _____
                            (nonvisual detail)

      _____ ,

    2   _____
                            (special detail)

      _____ .

6. 1   She raced across the court,

    2   _____
                            (visual detail)

      _____ ,

    2   _____
                            (special detail)

      _____ .

7. 1   He stood at the edge of the pool,

    2   _____
                            (nonvisual detail)

      _____ ,

    2   _____
                            (nonvisual detail)

      _____ .

8. 1   She came quietly down the steps,

    2   _____
                            (visual detail)

      _____ ,

    2   _____
                            (nonvisual detail)

      _____ .

9. 1   I could hear him down in his workshop,

    2   _____
                            (nonvisual detail)
         _____ ,

    2   _____
                            (special detail)
         _____ .

10. 1   He took a huge bite out of the pizza wedge,

    2   _____
                            (nonvisual detail)
         _____ ,

    2   _____
                            (nonvisual detail)
         _____ .

NARRATIVE DETAILS USING ABSOLUTE PHRASES

Using the absolute phrase is a second way to present narrative details. Often, the subject of the phrase will be the detail, and the predicate will usually begin with a present participial phrase. In the examples that follow, notice how the absolute phrases provide visual, nonvisual, or special details.

Visual details

    1   He began scrambling up the wooden pegs nailed to the side of the tree,
        2   his back muscles working like a panther's.   —John Knowles

    1   He watched [the stage coach] go by,
        2   the four horses spanking along as the driver flicked them,
        2   the polished metal gleaming in the sun,
        2   the body swaying as the wheels rose and fell in the rough trail.
                                  —A. B. Guthrie

    1   In his room Cal sat at his desk,
        2   elbows down,
        2   hands holding his aching head together,
        2   palms pushing against the sides of his head. —John Steinbeck

Nonvisual details

    1   He sat down beside her,
        2   the clean whiff of antiseptic soap filling the car as he banged shut
            the door.   —Helen Hull

    1   At my back the turntable whirred,
        2   the needle making a dull scrape among the last grooves.
                                    —Saul Bellow

    1   After that we rode on in silence,
        2   the traces creaking,
        2   the hooves of the horses clumping steadily in the soft sand,
        2   the grasshoppers shrilling from the fields and the cicadas from the
            trees overhead.   —E. W. Teale

Special details

    1   In a pause Rosemary looked away and up the table where Nichole sat
            between Tommy Barban and Abe North,
        2   her chow's hair foaming and frothing in the sunlight.
                                —F. Scott Fitzgerald

    1   He could see the stallion rolling away before him down the slope,
        2   its long and heavy tail and mane streaming,
            3   their flowing giving shape to the invisible wind. —Walter Van Tilburg Clark

Note: In the above sentence the second-level element uses the absolute phrase to carry a visual detail. The third-level absolute phrase, however, provides the special, highly imaginative detail.

NARRATION

Name:_____

EXERCISE B: details in absolute phrases   Accuracy _____ Creativity _____

Directions: In the following sentences, fill in each blank with an absolute phrase that provides either a visual detail, a nonvisual detail, or a special detail, as indicated. For the predicate, use a present participle.

1.   2   As the light turned green,

   1   he drove away,

     2   _____
        (visual detail)
        _____,

     2   _____
        (nonvisual detail)
        _____.

2.   1   By late afternoon she reached the top of the path,

     2   _____
        (nonvisual detail)
        _____,

     2   _____
        (special detail)
        _____.

3.   1   He held the book open with one hand,

     2   _____
        (visual detail)
        _____,

     2   _____
        (special detail)
        _____.

4. 1   She kicked her swimfins and went under smoothly,

    2   _____
                          (nonvisual detail)
    _____,

    2   _____
                          (nonvisual detail)
    _____,

    2   _____
                          (special detail)
    _____.

5. 1   Grandmother continued as before,

    2   _____
                          (visual detail)
    _____,

    2   _____
                          (nonvisual detail)
    _____.

6. 1   He slouched along at my side,

    2   _____
                          (visual detail)
    _____.

7. 1   She gazed over the edge of the canyon,

    2   _____
                          (visual detail)
    _____,

    2   _____
                          (nonvisual detail)
    _____.

8. 1   He slid the chess piece slowly to the next square,

    2   _____
                    (visual detail)

    _____ ,

    2   _____
                    (visual detail)

    _____ .

9. 1   They moved closer to the fire,

    2   _____
                    (special detail)

    _____ ,

    2   _____
                    (special detail)

    _____ .

10. 1   Her fingers moved over the keys,

    2   _____
                    (nonvisual detail)

    _____ .

MAKING COMPARISONS

Remember that a comparison makes a connection for your reader between the new action you are presenting and one that is familiar. Many of the comparisons in the example sentences use *like* or *as*. But you should look carefully at the other methods these good writers have found to express similarity of action. It sometimes seems daunting to create a new comparison, one that does not sound trite, forced, or verbose. However, when you do discover the apt phrase, the unique analogy, you will know that your effort has been worthwhile.

Comparison as part of the base clause: Like most other modifiers, a comparison may or may not be set off from what it is modifying. These three examples illustrate the comparison written as part of the base clause.

> Alice raised her hand as though she would hold him back with a rope of air.
> —John Steinbeck

> Her fingers slid down and along the ground under the piece of money with the grace and care they would have in lifting an egg from under a setting hen.
> —Eudora Welty

> The light top sand of the road was blowing like smoke along the ground.
> —Shirley Ann Grau

Comparison in a lower level: In this set of examples the comparison is included, without punctuation, in one of the lower levels.

> 1 She stood there,
> 2   looking at Caddy,
> 2   wringing her long hand as though it were attached to her wrist with a string.
> —William Faulkner

> 1 Jim passed her often in the street,
> 2   walking small-boy fashion with her hands in her pockets.
> —F. Scott Fitzgerald

> 1 They crossed the room slowly,
> 2   groping at the darkness as if they might be tearing cobwebs from some unseen wall.   —William Styron

Comparison set off by punctuation as a separate level: In this set of examples, the comparison is set off from the other elements of the sentence, operating at its own additional level of generality. The punctuation changes the intonation and thus emphasizes the comparison.

> 1 He sat down on his chair again,
> 2   as slowly as an old man whose bones are stiff. —Mark Schorer

1 I waved at Walt,

  2 smiling,

    3 the way girls do in illustrations.

          —Mavis Gallant

  1 Now it was time to move, and,

    2 as a woman gathers her things together, / , and gets up to go

        out of the theater into the street,

      3/ her cloak,

      3/ her gloves,

      3/ her opera glasses

  1 she rose from the sofa and went to Peter.

          —Virginia Woolf

NARRATION

Name:_____

EXERCISE C: comparisons

Accuracy _____ Creativity _____

Directions: In the following sentences, you are to fill in the blanks with comparisons. Some are part of the base clause, some are part of a lower level, and some are themselves a separate level.

1. Aunt Helen presided over the dinner table _____

    _____ .

2. 1   The bicyclist looked at the tire disgustedly,

    2   shaking his head from side to side _____

    _____ .

3. The exchange student handled her knife and fork _____

    _____ .

4. 1   He picked up the phone gingerly with his fingertips, _____

    2   _____ .

5. 1   She turned on the lights,

    2   her finger flicking the switch _____

    _____ .

6. My little brother threw himself on the bed _____

    _____ .

7. 1   The scholar carefully turned the stiff manuscript pages,

    2   _____

    _____ .

8. 1   Jessica held open the elevator door,

    2   motioning toward us _____

    _____ .

9. 1   The stage manager peeked around the edge of the curtain,

    2   _____

    _____ .

10. The math teacher looked at the test results _____

    _____ .

11. 1   The girl went up the stairs,

    2   dragging her feet_____

    _____ .

12. The victorious football team waved to the spectators _____

    _____ .

13. 1   He stood with one foot on the gunwale and the other on the dock,

    2   his muscles flexing smoothly with the rocking boat,

    3   _____

    _____ .

14. The chef shook the mashed potato from the spoon,

    2   his hand coming down _____

    _____ .

15. 1   She brought her pencil close to the multiple-choice boxes,

    2   the point hovering above the paper,

    3   _____

    _____ .

NARRATION

Name:_____

EXERCISE D: details to establish context

Accuracy _____ Creativity _____

Many times the details in a second-level element will do more than authenticate the action pictured in the main clause. The details will often establish the actual context or situation as well. For instance, in the following sentence the scene might take place on a dance floor.

> 1   He came toward them slowly,
> 2   holding his partner in an awkward embrace.

But it could also take place at a skating rink.

> 1   He came toward them slowly,
> 2   holding his skates by the laces.

Or it could take place on the street.

> 1   He came toward them slowly,
> 2   waving the car over to the curb.

Directions: For each sentence, we have supplied three possible contexts for the action. You are to complete each sentence using details that will suggest one of the situations.

1. 1.   He knelt down on one knee,

    2   holding _____

    _____ .

Possible situations: (1) He is a tourist. (2) He is fixing something. (3) He is playing with his grandchildren.

2. 1.   She went from one end of the room to the other,

    2   taking _____

    _____ .

Possible situations: (1) She is a waitress. (2) She is a hostess at a party. (3) She is cleaning up after painting her room

3. 1.   The man rose to his full height,

    2   getting _____

    _____ .

Possible situations: (1) The man is a store clerk. (2) He is watching a parade. (3) He is trying on new clothes.

4. 1. He sat directly across from me,

    2   looking _____

    _____ .

Possible situations: (1) He is waiting for a train. (2) He is studying. (3) We are having coffee together.

5. 1. She listened to their loud voices,

    2   moving _____

    _____ .

Possible situations: (1) She is an actress waiting for her cue. (2) She is trying to ignore an argument. (3) She is trying to attract the attention of the people speaking.

In the following set of sentences, you are to supply the entire second-level element, thereby establishing any context or situation you wish. Begin your second level with a present participle.

6. 1. He made his way up the steps,

    2   _____

    _____ .

7. 1. The fish went skittering away,

    2   _____

    _____ .

8. 1. He leaned over the desk,

    2   _____

    _____ .

9. 1. The little girl came into the room,

    2   _____

    _____ .

10. 1. She was obviously comfortable,

    2   _____

    _____ .

8. DESCRIPTION

SHARPENING THE IMAGE PROPOSED BY THE NOUN

You have learned that narrative writing focuses on the action, and the action is expressed through the verbs. Descriptive writing focuses on the people, places, things, and ideas among which that action occurs—in other words, description centers on the nouns.

The three methods of sharpening the image proposed by the verb, which we examined in Chapter 7, are exactly the same as those that will be used for sharpening the image proposed by the noun: adding detail, indicating a quality, and making a comparison. In the example sentence below, the author has used all three methods. The nouns being described appear in bold type, and the modifiers are in italics.

1   Only gradually one finds he too is learning the subtlest differences where at first all seems alike:

2   **the branches of ironwood**,

3   *like the muscles of a straining wrestler,*   **Comparison**

2   **the shape of elms** *like a falling fountain,*   **Comparison**

2   **the** *mottled* **bark of sycamores,**   **Quality**

2   **the alders** *with their little cones,*   **Detail**

2   **the hickories** *with their buds almost like flowers*— **Detail**

1   out of the silvery winter ranks individuals step forth, are marked, remembered.

—D. C. Peattie

In this example the author has been speaking about a forest and now uses a series of noun phrases to focus on the specific trees within the forest in order to point out their differences. The nouns *ironwood, elms, sycamores, alders,* and *hickories* operate at a lower level of generality to help the reader subdivide the forest. In turn, these nouns are being further described, using the three methods we have mentioned.

USING QUALITIES TO SHARPEN THE NOUN

We will begin with quality, because it is based on the simplest noun modifier, the adjective. The adjective *mottled* in the example illustrates this type of description. It describes the bark by providing a characteristic, or attribute, which helps us to visualize it better.

Most often, adjectives are placed in the bound position immediately before the noun they are describing. By removing them from this traditional position, however, and giving them their own levels of generality, we create an opportunity both to draw additional attention to the adjectives and to elaborate upon them with even further details, qualities, and comparisons.

Here are several sentences that demonstrate the technique of placing adjectives in lower levels of generality, as free modifiers of a noun in the base clause.

1   The mother heard his **boots**, / , and looked up at him.
2/   *hard* on the bare floor and then *heavy* on the piece of old carpet that
                did for a rug

—Walter Van Tilburg Clark

1   Don Antonio was a large **man**,
2   *heavy*,
2   *full* at the waist,
2   a trifle *bald*, and
2   very *slow* of speech.   —Willa Cather

In the next two sentences, the authors have clustered the adjectives in the same level of generality for the purposes of style and meaning.

1   Or else it was his seaweedy merman's **odor**,
2   mixed with the meatlike scorch of tobacco,
2   *strong* and *salty*.   —Cynthia Ozick

1   The enemy was a **toad** who sat by preference near the toolhouse door:
2   *obese*, *sage*, and *wrinkled* like a Chinese god.
—Conrad Aiken

Next is an example of a sentence in which each adjective has its own separate level. In addition, the author has used a comma to separate the final prepositional phrase comparison from the adjectives before it. This indicates that the phrase is intended to be a modifier of the three preceding adjectives. The punctuation also provides a rhythm to the sentence, which enhances the content.
    Notice this time that the noun being modified appears in the Level 2.

1   We waited in the shade [of the hangar],
2   listening to the **wind** outside,
3   *gentle*,
3   *persistent*,
3   *continuous*,
4   like a distant line of breakers.   —Anne Morrow Lindbergh

Note: A quality of a noun will always be designated by an adjective, but not all adjectives designate a quality. An adjective may also designate a detail, *oak-paneled*, or a comparison, *childlike* or *childish*. An abstract adjective, such as *beautiful*, does not picture at all but summarizes, and should be regarded as expository—explaining rather than describing. Instead, try to express the elements that make your noun beautiful, letting your reader experience the beauty firsthand.

DESCRIPTION

Name:_____

EXERCISE A: using qualities to describe

Accuracy _____ Creativity _____

Directions: Complete the following sentences by adding second-level adjectives to sharpen the image of the noun or pronoun printed in **bold** type. After the adjective, you may add additional information that you consider appropriate. Choose one of the suggestions to help you formulate the descriptions in your second-level elements.

Example: 1   He walked across the **lawn**,

2 _____.
   (Situation: after a shower; after an outdoor wedding reception; in need of mowing)

Possible responses: *spongy* from the sudden shower

or

messy with confetti and wind-blown paper plates

or

thick and *lush* as it awaited the mower

1.   1   The **toddlers** sat on the stairs,

2   _____
   (Situation: a party downstairs; Halloween; bedtime)

_____ .

2.   1   The new **girl**, /, played on the jungle gym.

2/   _____
   (Situation: her classmates had been friendly or hostile; the teacher had ignored her)

_____

3.   1   They forgot the **bacon**,

2   _____
   (Situation: left in the skillet; left in the car; how it smelled)

_____ .

4.   1   The **dishwasher**, / , grumbled through its chore,

2/   _____
   (Situation: in humorous terms; as if it were human)

_____

5. 1   **He** shuffled through the mail,

    2   _____

        (Situation: postman sorting his load; someone anxious for a special letter; a stamp collector)

    _____ .

6. 1   The **lamp**, / , stood on the corner of the desk.

    2/ _____

        (Describe: shape, color, size, brightness, or utility)

    _____

7. 1   The **bushes** were putting forth leaves,

    2   _____

        (Describe: how the leaves would look if the spring had been late or early, hot or cold)

    _____ .

8. 1   The **Thanksgiving turkey**, / , occupied the center of the table.

    2/ _____

        (Situation: size; how it looked; how it smelled)

    _____

9. 1   They stopped at a farmstand selling fresh **produce**,

    2   _____

        (Describe: smells, tastes, appearances)

    _____ .

10. 1   The young **girl** walked down the aisle,

    2   _____

        (Situation: at a wedding; in a store; in a theater)

    _____ .

USING DETAILS TO SHARPEN THE NOUN

Unlike qualities, which tell characteristics or attributes of nouns, descriptive details bring us closer, focusing on a smaller portion of the object or scene. The sentences that follow use a variety of grammatical constructions to carry descriptive details. The noun being described has been printed in bold type. Notice that the nouns and their descriptive details may appear at the lower levels, and that the use of details may combine with the other methods, of quality (*dark and shiny*) and comparison (*like mud*; *as little clam shells*).

Noun phrases used to carry descriptive detail

    1   The mist took pity on the fretted **structures** of earlier generations:
        2   the Post Office with its shingle-tortured mansard,
        2   the red brick minarets of hulking old houses,
        2   factories with stingy and sooted windows,
        2   wooden tenements colored like mud.   —Sinclair Lewis

Prepositional phrase used to carry descriptive detail

    1   His **hands** were hard,
        2   with broad fingers and nails as thick and ridged as little clam shells.
                    —John Steinbeck

Verb phrase used to carry descriptive detail

        2   In his apartment,
            3   the expensive, oak-paneled, high-ceilinged **place** in New York's upper Seventies,
                4   crusted with books and littered with ashtrays,
    1   she had lived out a life of chores, and
    1   tiny chores had lengthened before her like shadows drawn out into a sun slant; . . .   —Elizabeth Spencer

Absolute phrases used to carry descriptive detail

    1   In the front yard was a clump of tall **pines**,
        2   the rough brown trunks wet,
        2   the green branches, / , heavy with rain,
            3/   dark and shiny
        2   the ground underneath mournfully sodden and black.
                    —Ruth Suckow

Adjective clause used to carry descriptive detail

    1   In the spring of 1906 all the world skated,
        2   especially young **women** of leisure,
            3   who admired themselves in the tight fur-trimmed **jackets** and new ankle-length **skirts** ,
                4   which were worn with jaunty little caps in the skating-rinks.
                    —Ellen Glasgow

USING COMPARISONS TO SHARPEN THE NOUN

Comparison functions in the same manner in description as it does in narration. The only difference is that the author is comparing the image proposed by a noun rather than the image proposed by a verb. Only one of each type of comparison is illustrated, since the technique of comparison has been illustrated in the preceding chapter.

Comparison as part of the base clause

> Her face was lean and strong and her **eyes** were as clear as water.
> —John Steinbeck

Comparison in lower level

> 1 Her clear-looking eyes, / , were full of approval for Stephen.
> 2/   with fine little **rays** of brown in them like the spokes of a wheel
> —Katherine Anne Porter

Comparison set off as a separate level

> 1 The bright morning sky that day had a rare blue and white **fluffiness**,
> 2   as if a vacuum cleaner had raced across the heavens as a weekly,
>   clarifying duty.   —Elizabeth Hardwick

DESCRIPTION

Name:_____

EXERCISE B: using details to describe

Accuracy _____ Creativity _____

Directions: Fill in the blanks, using details to sharpen the image proposed by the noun printed in **bold** type.

Example: 1   She was the same young **woman** I had seen earlier,

2 ____ her hair pulled back in a jaunty ponytail and tied with a rubber band.
(absolute phrase)

1. 1   After dinner she looked over her host's CD **collection**,

2   _____
(noun phrase)

_____.

2. 1   The boy was undergoing the agony of adolescence—

2   his **arms**, /, _____.
(verb phrase)

3/ _____
(prepositional phrase)

3. 1   There at the bottom of his locker were his **sneakers**,

2   _____,
(absolute phrase)

2   _____.
(absolute phrase)

4. 1   The **meal**, / , was a never-to-be-forgotten experience.

2/ _____
(verb phrase)

_____.

5. 1   She stood wearily looking into the **refrigerator**,

2   _____
(adjective clause)

_____.

6. 1   He carried a basket full of **puppies**,

    2   _____ .
         (noun phrase)

7. 1   She wore an old **sweatshirt**,

    2   _____ .
         (absolute phrase)

8. 1   His father's reading **glasses**, / , lay in the ashtray.

    2/ _____
         (adjective clause)

9.   2   _____ ,
             (prepositional phrase)

    1   the **clowns** added interest and color to the parade.

10. 1   The **windows** were ugly,

    2   _____ .
         (verb phrase)

DESCRIPTION

Name:_____

EXERCISE C: using descriptive details

Accuracy _____ Creativity _____

Directions: Complete the following sentences by supplying second-level elements that carry descriptive details of the noun printed in **bold** type. You may use noun phrases, verb phrases, prepositional phrases, absolute phrases, or adjective clauses as the vehicles for the details. From the conditions suggested, choose one to help you formulate the descriptions in your second-level elements.

Example: 1   The roadside **diner** looked like a good place to have dinner,

2   <u>a neon "Open" sign blinking to the rhythm of the music coming from inside.</u>
(Describe: how it is lit; sounds or smells; what's on the menu)

1.   1   The **house** was on a sharp rise,

2   _____
(Describe: the view from the house; the view looking at the house; its position in the landscape)

_____ .

2.   1   She looked through the doorway of her friend's **room,**

2   _____
(Describe: decorations on wall; neatness of room; the window drapes or shades)

_____ .

3.   1   The **kitchen** was his favorite room,

2   _____
(Describe: the decor of the kitchen; the effect of the sunlight on the kitchen; the smells of the kitchen)

_____ .

4.   1   The **den**, / , was the most heavily used room in the house.

2/   _____
(Describe: its use as a television room; as a room with many functions; its handy location)

_____

5.   1   The **floral arrangement** sat in the middle of the table,

2   _____
(Describe: decorations on wall; neatness of room; the window drapes or shades)

_____ .

6.   1   She wore an unconvincing **smile**,

    2   _____

       (Describe: the edges of the smile; its disappearance and return; its artificial appearance)

    _____ .

7.   1   The garden **tools** had been put away,

    2   _____

       (Describe: how the tools were stored; how they showed much use; where they had been stored)

    _____ .

8.   1   The **car** was stuck in the slow lane,

    2   _____

       (Describe: the sound of the car; what was keeping it in the slow lane; the heating up of the car)

    _____ .

9.   1   The **dog** sprawled asleep in front of the fire,

    2   _____

       (Describe: the appearance of the firelight on the dog; its paws; its breathing)

    _____ .

10.   1   Reluctantly she threw out the **shoes**,

    2   _____

       (Describe: their condition after being neglected, after hard use, or after being used to paint in)

    _____ .

DESCRIPTION

Name:_____

EXERCISE D: using comparisons to describe

Accuracy _____ Creativity _____

Directions: Directions: In the following sentences, by using comparisons, you are to sharpen the image proposed by the noun printed in **bold** type. Some of the additions you make will be in the base clause, some will be in a lower level, and some will themselves be the lower-level element.

    Note: When creating comparisons, you should guard against those that are trite, inappropriate or incongruous, or clumsily worded. The comparison should be as original aspossible, and it ought to be simply and neatly phrased.

Example: 1   It was a wonderful old **car**,

            2   _____with seatcovers like my childhood security blanket_____ .

1. 1   He put on his father's **suit**,

      2   a hopelessly old-fashioned suit with lapels _____

        _____ .

2. 1   A sense of uneasy **expectancy**, / , hung over the classroom.

      2/ _____

        _____

3. 1   He set the tiles in an intricate **pattern**,

      2 _____

        _____ .

4. 1   The damp **fireworks** were _____

        _____ .

5. 1   The **ducklings** in the tall grass looked _____

        _____ .

6. 1   He rode a beat-up **motorcycle**,

      2 _____

        _____ .

7. 1   Thick **moss**, / , covered the side of the tree.

      2/ _____

        _____

8. 1   The ecstatic **fans** celebrated the goal,

    2   _____

    _____ .

9. 1   He watched the swinging **pendulum**,

    2   _____

    _____ .

10. 1   The piece of welded **sculpture**, / , stood in front of the new office building.

    2/   _____

    _____

EXERCISE E: descriptive details and comparisons   Accuracy _____ Creativity _____

Directions: The following sentences are to be used as first-level elements. Select one of the nouns in each sentence and supply a second-level element that sharpens the image proposed by that noun by detail, by comparison, or by both. Use your own paper for this exercise.

Example: 1   The repairman carried a large **toolbox**,
                  2   filled with spare parts and jars of nuts and bolts.   (detail)
                               or
                  2   its heavy wrenches jangling like a convict's chains.   (detail and comparison)

1. The Sunday paper was all over the living room.

2. The weather had been discouraging all summer.

3. The playground had an old swing set.

4. The man stared at the menu on the lunch counter.

5. The snow shovel was under the basement stairs.

6. The expressway was partly closed for repairs.

7. Everyone arrived at the prom drenched by the cloudburst.

8. A magazine salesman called on the phone.

9. Marvin barely touched the unfamiliar food.

10. The pile of get-well cards grew every day.

THE FREE NOUN PHRASE IN DESCRIPTIVE SENTENCES

By now you are familiar with the free noun phrase as a way of identifying and clarifying a noun in the base clause. The first noun is likely to be either general or abstract, and the added free noun phrase is usually more concrete and particular. As you know, such a free noun phrase is often called an *appositive*.

Writers will often expand upon a simple appositive for the purpose of description, adding modifiers and details that bring the image into sharper focus.

> 1   The **farmhouse** stood off among the trees,
>   2   a yellow shape with points here and there,
>   3   two red chimneys budding out of the roof.   —E. M. Roberts

In the next example a parallel series of noun phrases follows the base clause, each presenting a descriptive detail to sharpen the original generalization.

> 1   All the **magic** of Camusfearna was fixed in that morning:
>   2   the vivid lightning streak of an otter below water;
>   2   the wheeling, silver-shouldered flight of the geese as they passed to
>   alight ahead of us;
>   2   the long, lifting, blue swell of the sea among the skerries and the
>   sea tangle;
>   2   the little rivers of froth and crystal that spilled back from the rocks as
>   each smooth wave sucked back and left them bare.
>   —Gavin Maxwell

In the following example the base clause introduces a plural term. What follows then is a parallel series of noun phrases, each carrying a specific example of the original plural term.

> 1   Around Devon we had **gaits** of every description:
>   2   gangling shuffles from boys who had suddenly grown a foot taller
>   2   swinging cowboy lopes from those thinking how wide their shoulders
>   had become,
>   2   ambles,
>   2   waddles,
>   2   light trippings,
>   2   gigantic Bunyan strides.
>   —John Knowles

ADDITIONAL NOUN PHRASE TECHNIQUES

The following three examples illustrate some additional effects that can be achieved with thoughtful application of the noun phrase.

First, you should notice how the authors of all three sentences move freely between narrative and descriptive writing, moving ahead one moment to tell something that happened, then pausing the next to describe the scene more vividly. Such ebb and flow is at the heart of all good creative writing.

In the first sentence, the author demonstrates the noun phrase technique of direct repetition of the noun in the base clause, *tie*. Such a device, though not to be overused, can lend a feeling of logic, symmetry, or drama to your writing.

> 1 The little man pulled at the top of his **tie** ,
> 2 a small blue **tie** with red polka dots,
> 3   slightly frayed at the knot.
>
> —Katherine Anne Porter

The next sentence demonstrates a variation on the principle of levels of generality. While most lower-level elements are more specific than the ones above them, here the movement is in the opposite direction, from specific to general, from *dolphins* to *fish*.

> 1 A few hours later we caught two small **dolphins**,
> 2 startlingly beautiful **fish** of pure gold,
> 3   pulsing and fading and changing colors.   —John Steinbeck

The final example shows how a noun phrase can be used to sharpen an image proposed, not by a noun, but by some other grammatical element. That element might be an adjective, a verb, or, as here, an infinitive.

> 1 The forward guywire of our mast began **to sing** under the wind,
> 2 a deep and yet penetrating **tone** like the lowest string of an incredible bullfiddle.
>
> —John Steinbeck

DESCRIPTION

Name:_____

EXERCISE F: descriptive noun phrases—part 1

Accuracy _____ Creativity _____

Directions: In each of the blanks provided, you are to write a noun phrase in apposition to the noun printed in **bold** type. The noun phrase should restate in a more specific way the given noun. Having written the appositive, you may then add additional bound modifiers that would further enhance your description.

Example: 1 It was an unexpected **delight**,
             2 _____ *the sound of children outside singing carols.*_____

1. 1   It was a graduation **present** from his father,

    2   _____

        _____ .

2. 1   The **room** was in keeping with its occupant—

    2   _____ ,

    2   _____ , and

    2   _____ .

3. 1   The **plant** threatened to take over one end of the room,

    2   _____

        _____ .

4. 1   The **back porch** was a stage for all their games,

    2   _____

        _____ .

5. 1   The **vendor** moved up the aisle toward them,

    2   _____ .

6. 1   They picked up the picnic **clutter**,

    2   _____ ,

    2   _____ .

7.   1   In the end seat three **commuters** were playing cards,

       2   _____ ,

       2   _____ , and

       2   _____ .

8.   1   The dry cleaner checked the **clothes** on his rack,

       2   _____ ,

       2   _____ ,

       2   _____ .

9.   1   The orchestra's **instruments** were already packed,

       2   _____ ,

       2   _____ ,

       2   _____ .

10. 1   **Loneliness** swept over him as the plane disappeared into a cloud,

       2   _____

       _____ .

DESCRIPTION

Name:_____

EXERCISE G: descriptive noun phrases—part 2   Accuracy _____ Creativity_____

Directions: In each of the blanks provided, you are to write a noun phrase that begins with a noun in apposition to the image proposed by the word or words printed in bold type. Try out some of the additional techniques described earlier—the direct repetition of the noun, the movement to a more general noun, or the expression in noun form of an image proposed by a verb, adjective, or infinitive.

Example: 1 He looked at the **snake** in the fifty-gallon terrarium,
                  2 _____*a monster right out of his worst nightmare.*_____

1. 1   To save time he ordered the **quick-lunch special**,

   2   _____

   _____.

2. 1   He **dived** at the ball carrier,

   2   _____

   _____.

3. 1   The movers **struggled** with the big chair,

   2   _____

   _____.

4. 1   They slammed the heavy rear doors of the **moving van**,

   2   _____

   _____.

5. 1   The sun-browned beachcombers returned with an assortment of **shells and driftwood**,

   2   _____

   _____.

6. 1   Then my front tire began to **hiss**,

   2   _____

   _____.

7. 1   They made a survey of the village's **poverty**,

    2   _____

    _____ .

8. 1   He **clowned** his way through school,

    2   _____

    _____ .

9. 1   The robins were **teaching** their fledglings to fly,

    2   _____

    _____ .

10. 1   The Chinese soup was both **sweet and sour,**

    2   _____

    _____ .

EXERCISE F: descriptive noun phrases—
      part 3
                           Accuracy _____ Creativity _____

Directions: In the following exercise, you are to select a noun, a verb, or an adjective in the narrative base sentence, underline the selected item, and then develop it with one or more second-level noun phrases. You may also add a third-level element, which need not be a noun phrase. Remember that you are describing the image proposed by the word you choose. Use your own paper for this exercise.

1. The applause was as varied as the audience.

2. The freighter was being unloaded at the dock.

3. The gangling boy fell over the footstool.

4. The vacuum cleaner gave out a little wheeze.

5. The baton twirler high-stepped down the street.

6. The students scuffed down the hall.

7. A bus jammed full of passengers whizzed past.

8. The exhausted workers carried the supplies into the already full storeroom.

9. The chauffeur kept looking for a parking space.

10. The caddy and the foursome trudged across the sun-drenched golf course.

9. EXPOSITION

The expository sentence, which you will be studying and writing in this chapter, does not attempt to picture an action—as the narrative sentence does. Nor does it attempt to picture people or objects—as the descriptive sentence does. Instead, the expository sentence tries to make you understand. To put it another way, the aim of both narration and description is to make you see and feel. The aim of exposition is to explain.

In narrative and descriptive writing, the sentence is the basic unit of composition. You have explored ways to make an individual image sharp, knowing that the chronology of your story would provide the overall unity as you moved from one scene to another.

In expository writing, however, the basic unit of composition is the paragraph. Usually, there will not be a simple chronology to unite your ideas, so you will need to find other ways to ensure that your reader follows your presentation. One important step is to get off to a good start.

You are probably familiar with the terms **topic sentence** for a paragraph and **thesis statement** for an essay. They are the sentences that tell your reader what the paragraph or essay will be about. In addition to informing your reader of the content, a well-constructed opening sentence can also provide an overview of how you will be developing your ideas. By using the principles of addition and levels of generality in expository writing, both in sentences and in paragraphs, you will find that the essay is easier for you to write and for the reader to understand.

In this chapter we will present a number of ways to construct the lower levels of generality in an expository sentence so that you will have a firm foundation on which to develop the rest of your essay. Care and thought at this stage will help prepare you for the writing of paragraphs, which is discussed in the final chapter.

THE EXPOSITORY SENTENCE WITH A SINGLE SECOND-LEVEL ELEMENT

In the expository sentence—as was true of both the narrative and the descriptive sentence— the second-level element treats in a more specific way material that was dealt with in an abstract or general way in the base clause.

Here are three examples of expository sentences that have only one Level 2.

1   In all learning there is a radical pioneering force and a conservative supporting force,
  2   a learning that explores and a learning that consolidates.
              —Northrop Frye

1   In recent years the machine has been perfected to perform uncanny tasks,
  2   the most striking being the calculation and solution of involved mathematical problems.
    —S. I. Hayakawa

1   A prejudice is a *pre*judgment,
  2   a conclusion reached *before* any real evidence is in.
              —W. W. Watt

It might be useful to imagine that the base clause positions you, and your reader, in front of a set of doors. It establishes the topic for discussion, but gives little indication of the direction that discussion will follow. With the Level 2 you reach out your hand, turn the knob on one of the doors, and step through. Think about this image as you read the following sentences.

> 1   We rarely profit from our mistakes,
>   2   mistakes which often result in war after war with only intermittent
>   periods of peace.

From the many doors offered by the opening statement, this author has chosen to explore the topic from a global and historical perspective. A strong cause-and-effect relationship is established by the word *result*, and the overall tone of the paragraph will probably be serious.

The second level in the preceding example uses the most basic of noun phrase techniques, the direct repetition of the noun *mistakes* from the Level 1.

Here is another way that the same base clause might be developed.

> 1   We rarely profit from our mistakes,
>   2   making the old ones over again but giving them new names.

This time the lower-level modifier, a present participial phrase, sets up a possible approach for the rest of the paragraph based on contrast, the old mistakes and their new names. The tone might be serious, as *war* becomes *peacekeeping action*. Or the tone might be playful, as *fat* becomes *circumferentially challenged*. Quite different doors!

In the next example, an absolute phrase attempts to explain why the statement offered in the base clause is true.

> 1   We rarely profit from our mistakes,
>   2   emotion being more powerful than reason.

With this beginning, one author might launch a debate between religious fundamentalism and Darwinism, while another could discuss the wisdom of following fashion trends or buying more practical clothes.

The final example uses a subordinate clause as the free modifier.

> 1   We rarely profit from our mistakes,
>   2   unless it is to make bigger ones.

This statement seems to offer the most cynical view of all. Yet, depending on the examples that come later in the paragraph, the result could range from serious historical analysis to biting satire to absurd silliness. The choice is yours.

EXPOSITION

Name:_____

EXERCISE A: the single second-level element

Accuracy _____ Creativity _____

Directions: In each of the following sentences, you are to narrow the focus of the base clause by supplying a single second-level element. This element can be of any grammatical construction. Be prepared to discuss what direction the remainder of your paragraph might take.

1.   1   Dating can be looked upon as a game,

        2 _____

           _____

           _____ .

2.   1   Every teacher knows that many things besides school compete for a student's attention,

        2 _____

           _____

           _____ .

3.   1   Cars are usually advertised as more than just a means of transportation,

        2 _____

           _____

           _____ .

4.   1   So often, things could be made better with an apology,

        2 _____

           _____

           _____ .

5.   1   Students know that homework is assigned for many reasons,

        2 _____

           _____

           _____ .

6.   1   Depending on nature means different things to different people,

      2   _____

          _____

          _____ .

7.   1   One's tastes rarely remain the same over time,

      2   _____

          _____

          _____ .

8.   1   My notion of "having enough money" differs from yours,

      2   _____

          _____

          _____ .

9.   1   Not all frontiers are physical,

      2   _____

          _____

          _____ .

10. 1   Sometimes we unwisely reckon costs only in terms of dollars and cents,

      2   _____

          _____

          _____ .

THE EXPOSITORY SENTENCE WITH A
SIMPLE COORDINATE SEQUENCE

The following sentences are examples of the expository sentence with a simple coordinate sequence. A simple coordinate sequence has only second-level elements after the base clause, and always more than one of them.

1   This book is about the English language—
     2   its nature,
     2   its history,
     2   its vocabulary,
     2   its writing system,
     2   and to some degree its use.   —W. Nelson Francis

1   Some of our failures are due to causes we have already noticed—
     2   our prejudices which lead us to distort the evidence,
     2   our keeping our minds in blinkers and thus closed against criticism and incapable of further reflection,
     2   our habit of using words repeated parrot-fashion,
     2   and our fear of being dragged from the shelter of our comforting beliefs.
       —L. S. Stebbins

The above examples differ from the sentences in the previous section in a number of ways. The sentence about the English language might appear at the beginning of an essay, offering a possible clue as to how the essay might develop; but the second example is clearly placed well into a longer discussion, as revealed by the phrase "causes we have already noticed." The Level 2 noun phrases here offer a summary of information that has gone before, in anticipation of a turning point in the larger essay.

Thus the purpose of the simple coordinate sequence is usually not to set a tone or to present an attitude toward the subject matter. Instead, the free modifiers will often imply a structure that the paragraph will follow, summarize the argument to that point, or break down a complex concept into smaller, more manageable components. This structure can provide a point of focus within your essay.

Also, you should notice in the above examples the technique of expressing **similar things in similar ways**. Both sentences rely on a series of second-level noun phrases, as well as direct repetition of the introductory words—*its* and *our*. When you write expository prose, look for ways in which you can present your ideas in a form that will emphasize order, clarity, and logic. Becoming skilled with such techniques will also make you a better reader, as you learn to recognize the methods being used by other good writers.

THE EXPOSITORY SENTENCE WITH A SIMPLE SUBORDINATE SEQUENCE

The expository sentence with a simple subordinate sequence also has multiple levels, but the elements, instead of being all on the second level, or *coordinate*, are now *subordinate*. This means that each sentence element below the base clause is at a lower level than the preceding one.

1   Grammar [traditionally] was thought of as the art of speaking and writing correctly—
    2   an art expressed in a set of terms and distinctions which did not require severe examination,
        3   since they were firmly established and were presumed to be generally applicable.

—James Sledd

1   What Maitland has called the heroic age of English legal scholarship was soon to begin,
    2   launched by the great antiquaries,
        3   the collectors and expositors of manuscripts—
            4   Cotton, Bodley, Camden, Spelman, Selden, D'Ewes, and the rest.

—Catherine Drinker Bowen

1   But of course the real barriers to break down were those between the three major divisions of education,
    2   the elementary, secondary, and university levels,
        3   each of which tends to become a self-endorsed system,
            4   congratulating itself on its virtues and blaming whatever deficiencies the educational process as a whole may have on the other systems.   —Northrop Frye

EXPOSITION

Name:_____

EXERCISE B: simple coordinate sequence

Accuracy _____ Creativity _____

Directions: In each of these sentences, you are to develop the meaning by supplying second-level elements, treating in a more specific manner what is stated in a general way in the base clause.

1. 1   In the novel *The Caine Mutiny*, by Herman Wouk, a character claims that the navy is run according to a plan invented by geniuses for idiots:

      2   by geniuses _____

          _____

          _____ ,

      2   for idiots _____

          _____ .

2. 1   In each of us the dreamer and the practical one live side by side,

      2   the dreamer _____

          _____

          _____ ,

      2   the practical one _____

          _____

          _____ ,

      2   each _____

          _____

          _____ .

3. 1   In the course of a single day, the high school student plays many different roles:

      2   _____

          _____

          _____ ,

      2   _____

          _____

          _____ ,

      2   _____

          _____ .

4. 1   In some respects both academic failure and business failure have the same roots:

       2   an inability to _____

           _____

           _____ , and

       2   an unwillingness to _____

           _____

           _____ .

5. 1   Only a child or a naive person believes the popular myths about scientists,

       2   that they _____

           _____

           _____ ,

       2   that they_____

           _____

           _____ , and

       2   that they_____

           _____

           _____ .

6. 1   We can point out a number of shortcomings in the legal system:

       2   _____

           _____

           _____ ,

       2   _____

           _____

           _____ , and

       2   _____

           _____

           _____ .

7. 1   In our essentially nonreligious society, quite a few people worship a collection of false gods:

     2   _____

         _____

         _____ ,

     2   _____

         _____

         _____ , and

     2   _____

         _____

         _____ .

8. 1   Any student new to a school automatically has certain problems—

     2   _____

         _____

         _____ ,

     2   _____

         _____

         _____ , and

     2   _____

         _____

         _____ .

9. 1   A young child has certain basic needs—

     2   _____

         _____

         _____ ,

     2   _____

         _____

         _____ , and

     2   _____

         _____

         _____ .

10. 1   Extracurricular activities perform several vital functions for students:

    2   _____

        _____

        _____ ,

    2   _____

        _____

        _____ , and

    2   _____

        _____

        _____ .

11. 1   My family always has trouble deciding where we should go on spring break—

    2   somewhere _____

        _____

        _____ , or

    2   somewhere _____

        _____

        _____ .

12. 1   At any sporting event there are basically two kinds of spectators,

    2   _____

        _____

        _____ , and

    2   _____

        _____

        _____ .

EXPOSITION

Name:_____

EXERCISE C: simple subordinate sequence

Accuracy _____ Creativity _____

Directions: In the following sentences, you are to fill in the blanks with whatever grammatical constructions you feel are appropriate, thus creating a sentence based on the simple subordinate sequence. Each lower-level item will treat in a more specific and concrete way what is presented in the next higher level of generality.

1.   1   So the job hunter begins _____
_____
_____ ,

       2   _____
_____
_____ ,

       3   _____
_____
_____ .

2.   1   The _____ often finds herself torn
between two _____ ,

       2   _____ and
_____ ,

       3   each_____
_____
_____ ,

       4   _____
_____ .

3.   1   _____ in a ticklish situation knows
enough to _____ ,

       2   _____ and
_____
_____ ,

       3   _____
_____
_____ .

4. 1 _____ seldom has time

to _____ ,

2 _____

_____

_____ ,

3 _____

_____

_____ .

5. 1 _____ dislike(s)

having to _____ ,

2 _____

_____

_____ ,

3 _____

_____

_____ .

6. 1 _____ represents a turning point in one's life,

2 _____

_____

_____ ,

3 _____

_____

_____ .

7. 1 The _____ misses a great deal,

2 _____

_____

_____ ,

3 _____

_____

_____

_____ .

8. 1   The difference between _____ and

_____ is very real,

    2   _____

_____

_____ ,

        3   _____

_____

_____ .

9. 1   Too often in our schools we neglect _____ ,

    2   _____

_____

_____ ,

        3   _____

_____

_____ .

10. 1   The function of _____ is a crucial one,

    2   _____

_____

_____ ,

        3   _____

_____

_____ .

11. 1   A good hobby can _____

_____ ,

    2   _____

_____

_____ ,

        3   _____

_____

_____ .

12. 1 Setting personal goals helps _____

_____ ,

    2 _____

_____

_____ ,

      3 _____

_____

_____ .

THE EXPOSITORY SENTENCE WITH A MIXED SEQUENCE

You have now learned to use the expository sentence with a coordinate sequence and with a subordinate sequence. But most writers use a combination of these two to make a *mixed sequence*. In sentences with a mixed sequence, either the coordinate sequence or the subordinate sequence may provide the dominant pattern.

Mixed coordinate sequence

A mixed coordinate sequence will move to levels beyond the second level but will return to add one or more second-level elements. The clear intent, as established in the base clause, is to present a coordinate, or related, series of ideas, often expressed in similar ways.

> 1   We all live in two realities:
>   2   one of seeming fixity,
>   3   with institutions, dogmas, rules of punctuation, and routines,
>   4   the calendared and clockwise world of all-but-futile round and round;
>   2   and one of whirling and flying electrons, dreams, and possibilities,
>   3   behind the clock.   —Sidney Cox

>   2   Trusting his intuition,
> 1   he [Faulkner] wrote those stories which seemed to him at the time to have most interest and meaning,
>   2   letting the collage grow,
>   2   often doubling back in time to supply earlier episodes,
>   3   to which existing episodes became sequels,
>   2   leaving gaps to be filled someday,
>   2   starting sagas and putting them aside to start others,
>   2   brooding over his private world,
>   3   not so much as its creator as the medium through which it was trying to be created.
>   —Robert Coughlan

Mixed subordinate sequence

A mixed subordinate sequence will repeat an element at some levels beyond the base clause, but the clear intent is to move the reader through a progressively more specific series of ideas, images, or points.

> 1   Scholars whose predecessors had created the tools for analyzing equilibrium and stability have had to modify those instruments and deal with change—
>   2   economic, social, political change,
>   3   all happening at once, and
>   3   each kind related to the others.
>   —Carnegie Corp. of New York *Quarterly*

107

1   The Tuscan villa, / , was becoming—briefly—a bower of bliss,
    2/   which was basically a fortified farmhouse
    2   a place of voluntary exile from the iron and stone of the counting house
        and piazza,
    2   especially for the rich, aggressive members of the middle class,
      3   the "fat popolani,"
      3   to whose estates succeeded, / , a new set of well-to-do refugees,
        4/   hundreds of years later
        4   the foreigners of the villa around Fiesola.

—Mary McCarthy

EXPOSITION

Name:_____

EXERCISE D: mixed sequences

Accuracy _____ Creativity _____

Directions: In the following sentences, you are to fill in the blanks with whatever grammatical constructions you feel are appropriate, thus creating a sentence based on the mixed sequence.

1. 1   Increasingly the graduating high school senior must make an uncomfortable choice—

    2   _____ ,

       3   _____ ,

    2   or _____ ,

       3   with _____ ,

          4   _____

            _____ .

2. 1   It probably is a myth that Americans want to _____

    _____ ,

    2   _____

       _____ ,

       3   _____

          _____ , and

       3   _____

          _____ .

3. 1   Today _____ (is/are)

    faced with two choices when _____

    _____ ,

    2   _____

       _____ (and/or)

    2   _____

       _____ ,

       3   _____

          _____ .

4. 1 _____ often overlook one of the most important

functions of _____ ,

     2 _____

_____ ,

       3 _____

_____ .

5. 1 Many _____ seem to be able to recognize only two

_____ ,

     2 _____ (and/or)

     2 _____ ,

       3 _____

_____ , and

       3 _____

_____ .

6. 1 A common characteristic of _____ is that

_____ ,

     2 _____

_____ ,

       3 _____

_____ ,

     2 _____

_____ .

7. 1 We can no longer be certain about _____

_____ ,

     2 _____

_____ ,

       3 _____

_____ , and

       3 _____

_____ .

8.   1   More than likely our society will continue to _____

_____ ,

    2   _____

_____ ,

        3   _____

_____ ,

        3   _____

_____ .

9.   1   Unfortunately, we have concerned ourselves mainly with the financial costs of

_____ ,

    2   _____

_____ , and

    2   _____

_____ ,

        3   _____

_____ .

10. 1   The language a person uses is a good indication of _____

_____ ,

    2   _____

_____ ,

        3   _____

_____ ,

    2   _____

_____ .

11. 1   Today _____ and

_____ have much the same problem,

   2   (what/how) _____

_____ ,

      3   _____

_____ ,

      3   _____

_____ .

12. 1   A child's endless questions serve _____

_____ ,

   2   _____

_____ ,

      3   _____

_____ , and

   2   _____

_____ ,

      3   _____

_____ ,

         4   _____

_____

_____ .

10. THE PARAGRAPH

Now that you are familiar with writing a wide variety of sentence structures using the principles of **addition** and **levels of generality**, it should be easy to make the transition to writing a similar variety of paragraph structures. Take a moment to think about the patterns, the levels, the ebb and flow that take place within a finely crafted cumulative sentence. Now, mentally snap your fingers and allow each of those levels to become itself a complete sentence within a paragraph. The Level 1 easily becomes the topic sentence, and the lower-level free modifiers become sentences that serve to support, explain, or develop the original assertion.

Studies of actual expository writing have shown that the topic sentence is nearly always at or near the beginning of the paragraph. Sometimes it is the shortest sentence in the paragraph; sometimes it is a question. Its purpose is to alert the reader to the idea the other sentences in the paragraph will address. And it is important that the writer remembers and stays on the course that the topic sentence has set.

THE SIMPLE COORDINATE SEQUENCE

In the previous chapter, "Exposition," you examined and wrote cumulative sentences in which the additions to the base clause consisted of a series of second-level elements. We called such a series a **simple coordinate sequence**.

In expository writing, paragraphs, too, can be based on a simple coordinate sequence of elements. Here are two examples of such paragraphs. The opening sentence establishes the topic, and the lower-level sentences, which begin in similar ways, provide more specific details.

1   In the names of justice, good sportsmanship, and general honesty, it is simply essential that information reported in the public press, in meetings or committees, or across lunch tables be double-checked.

    2   In engineering and industry this is a matter of profits or bankruptcy.

    2   In medicine it is a matter of life and death.

    2   In public affairs and in private life it is a matter of integrity or corruption.

    2   In the laboratory it is taken for granted as a necessary and elementary part of scientific behavior.

—Wendell Johnson

1   Apart from teaching him Latin, Stratford grammar school taught Shakespeare nothing at all.

    2   It did not teach him mathematics or any of the natural sciences.

    2   It did not teach him history, unless a few pieces of information about ancient events strayed in through Latin quotations.

    2   It did not teach him geography, for the first (and most inadequate) textbook on geography did not appear until the end of the century, and maps and atlases were rare even in university circles.

    2   It did not teach him modern languages, for when a second language was taught at a grammar school it was invariably Greek.

—Marchette Chute

Sometimes a paragraph that is part of a larger whole will take a sentence or two to relate itself to the material that has gone before. The topic sentence therefore becomes delayed. When it does finally appear, it can then be followed by a simple coordinate sequence of sentences which develop the thought presented in the topic sentence. The passage below illustrates this process.

1 Substantially, then, the empire of Henry II remained in extent as he found it at his accession to the English throne at the age of twenty-one.

 2 Accordingly it is not as a conqueror but as a ruler that he can lay claim to greatness.

  3 But although Henry attempted little in the way of acquiring new territory, he did much to consolidate his possessions and to extend his European power and influence.

   4 His daughters were married to the greatest princes of their time, Henry the Lion, duke of Saxony and Bavaria, King Alphonso VIII of Castile, King William II of Sicily.

   4 He made an alliance with the ruler of Provence and planned a marriage with the house of Savoy that would have given him control of the passes into Italy.

   4 He took his part in the struggle of Pope and anti-Pope, of Pope and Emperor; he corresponded with the emperor of Constantinople, refused the crown of the kingdom of Jerusalem, and died on the eve of his departure on a crusade.

—Charles Homer Haskins

THE PARAGRAPH

EXERCISE A: simple coordinate
                  sequence–part 1

Name:_____

Accuracy _____ Creativity _____

Directions: For each of the following base sentences, you are to supply either three or four second-level sentences.

To show that the sentences are coordinate, pattern them alike. In other words, let them all have the same grammatical structure. Nothing but confusion will be gained by varying the pattern of the sentences, especially the sentence beginnings.

Use your own paper for these paragraphs. Indent and number your sentences to show the levels of generality as you have done before for the parts of the sentence.

1. However much a person dreams of excelling, there is no way to achieve excellence except through training.

2. Added responsibility usually develops your known abilities and often uncovers still others you did not know you had.

3. Now and then everything seems to come into at least a temporary balance, as if you had reached a plateau where you could pause for a deep breath.

4. A family building a house builds itself into it.

5. Books have always been many things to the thoughtful individual.

THE PARAGRAPH

Name:_____

EXERCISE B:　　simple coordinate
　　　　　　　　sequence–part 2

Accuracy _____ Creativity _____

Directions: The following quotations are to be used as the base for the opening sentence of a paragraph that has a simple coordinate sequence. You can introduce them by a statement such as, "Shakespeare was right when he said, 'Sweet are the uses of adversity,' " or you can disagree with the author or express reservations about the statement. If you wish, you may use only part of the quotation. Use your own paper for this exercise.

Example:　　　　"Sweet are the uses of adversity."—Shakespeare

1　　Shakespeare was right when he said, "Sweet are the uses of adversity," because adversity can give rise to the growth of compassion, humility, and humor.

2　　No one deprived of his free-swinging stride for any length of time can ever again feel impatience at being trapped behind a hobbling person on a crowded street.

2　　No one forced into contemplative idleness by a mild but drawn-out illness can summon up his former intensity of complaint after he has seen the courage of the gravely ill.

2　　No one who has had a broken finger, splinted and bandaged, has ever found a doorway wide enough to pass through without being bumped.

1.　"Solitude is as needful to the imagination as society is wholesome to the character."
　　—James Russell Lowell

2.　"Nothing really matters but living—accomplishments are the ornaments of life, they come second."
　　—Willa Cather

3.　"Even when laws have been written down, they ought not always to remain unaltered."
　　—Aristotle

4.　"We teachers can only help the work going on, as servants wait upon a master."
　　—Maria Montessori

5.　"Inconsistencies of opinion, arising from changed circumstances, are often justifiable."
　　—Daniel Webster

6.　"Being taken for granted can be a compliment. It means you've become a comfortable, trusted element in another person's life."—Joyce Brothers

7.　"We could never learn to be brave and patient if there were only joy in the world." —Helen Keller

8.　"One ought, every day at least, to hear a little song, read a good poem, see a fine picture, and, if possible, to speak a few reasonable words."—Johann W. Goethe

9.　"Pioneers were the original rugged individualists, and from them we have inherited many of our ideals."
　　—Lloyd Garrison

10. "Every great mistake has a halfway moment, a split second when it can be recalled and perhaps remedied."
　　—Pearl S. Buck

THE SIMPLE SUBORDINATE SEQUENCE

An expository paragraph, like a sentence, can also be based on a subordinate sequence of elements, in which each element consists of a sentence rather than a free modifier. In a **simple subordinate sequence** there is no sentence that is coordinate with any sentence above or below it. Each succeeding sentence is linked to the one above it, but is at a lower level of generality.

1   Throughout our school years we were always keenly conscious of the growing development of Rockford Seminary into a college.
   2   The opportunity for our Alma Mater to take her place in the new movement of full college education for women filled us with enthusiasm, and it became a driving ambition with the undergraduates to share in this new and glorious undertaking.
     3   We gravely decided that it was important that some of the students should be ready to receive the bachelor's degree the very first moment that the charter of the school should secure the right to confer it.
       4   Two of us, therefore, took a course in mathematics, advanced beyond anything previously given in the school, from one of those early young women working for a Ph.D., who was temporarily teaching in Rockford that she might study more mathematics in Leipzig.

                                      —Jane Addams

1   Instead, the Boston Associates resolved to create a labor force that would be a shining example of those ultimate Yankee ideals: profit and virtue, doing good and doing well.
   2   This they accomplished for more than a generation by attracting a special class of temporary help.
     3   From the farms of Massachusetts, Vermont, New Hampshire, and Maine came robust young women, lured by the highest wages offered to female employees anywhere in America—from $1.85 to $3.00 a week, depending on skill and speed.
       4   This seemingly generous scale represented a considerable saving for the mill owners, since male mill workers were paid twice as much.   —Benita Eisler

117

1   The humanities, whatever is meant by that baffling term, seem to the musing observer to offer a succession of paradoxes.
2   The word itself is a modern invention, coming to us from the nineteenth century.
3   One might reasonably infer that, given so recent a coinage, we must know what we mean by it.
4   In fact, however, we do not quite know what we mean by it, and this is the first paradox.
5   We believe in something we cannot delimit.
6   Probably the only safe working definition is this: You know horses—cows are different.
7   You know the sciences, the humanities are different.
8   They are what you have left in the college curriculum when you extract the sciences—natural, physical, and social.

—Howard Mumford Jones

THE PARAGRAPH

Name:_____

EXERCISE C: simple subordinate
sequence—part 1

Accuracy _____ Creativity _____

Directions: For each of the following sentences, you are to supply at least three supporting sentences, each one a comment on or development of the sentence immediately before it. To show that each sentence is subordinate, you must vary the pattern from one sentence to another. By repeating words or by using pronouns or other connective words (*thus*, *therefore*, etc.) make it clear that the sentence you are writing refers to the one preceding it. Use your own paper for this exercise, and number the levels of generality as you have done before.

1. Movies today are better than ever.

2. Probably the happiest moment in the preparation for any major holiday or social event is when everyone discovers that it is time to stop fussing.

3. A few hours spent with a person who is enthusiastic and well-informed about a hobby can open a whole new world of discovery for us.

4. Astronomy has always fascinated me.

5. Good company makes a good evening.

THE PARAGRAPH

Name:_____

EXERCISE D: simple subordinate
                sequence–part 2

Accuracy _____ Creativity _____

Directions: The following quotations are to be used as the base for the opening sentence of a paragraph that has a simple subordinate sequence. You can introduce them by a statement such as, "Whitehead was right when he said, 'It requires a very unusual mind to undertake the analysis of the obvious,' " or you may disagree with the author or express reservations about the statement. If you wish, you may use only part of the quotation.

    Use your own paper for this exercise.

Example: "It requires a very unusual mind to undertake the analysis of the obvious."

— Alfred North Whitehead

1   Whitehead described one essential characteristic of the true innovator or researcher when he said, "It requires a very unusual mind to undertake the analysis of the obvious."
2   It is a mind at once impatient with anything that is self-evident, yet sufficiently patient to question the absurdly unquestionable.
3   This tenacious mind willingly endures the scoffers, admitting often that it does not know what it is doing, but feeling its way toward an answer that it knows intuitively must be there.
4   And eventually it almost seems to stumble upon a new synthesis of ideas as an accidental by-product of its main endeavor, a "Eureka!" moment that links this mind to the mind of Archimedes.

x1.   "Nothing is stronger than custom."—Ovid

2.   "Without music, life would be a mistake."—Friedrich Nietzsche

3.   "The seed never explains the flower."—Edith Hamilton

4.   "What we call failure is not the falling down, but the staying down."—Mary Pickford

5.   "You must learn to be still in the midst of activity and to be vibrantly alive in repose."—Indira Gandhi

6.   "Youth is wholly experimental."—Robert Louis Stevenson

7.   "How can one gauge friendship, save by its jewel-like rarity?"—Colette

8.   "The principal foundations of all states are good laws and good arms; and there cannot be good laws where there are not good arms."—Niccolò Machiavelli

9.   "Social misery has inspired the comfortably-off with the urge to take pictures, the gentlest of predations, in order to document a hidden reality, that is, a reality hidden from them." —Susan Sontag

10. "What the world will be like a century hence was never so impossible to foresee."—F. L. Lucas

THE MIXED SEQUENCE

Although, as you have seen in preceding sections, writers do write paragraphs based on simple coordinate or subordinate sequences, they are more likely to write paragraphs that are a combination of the two—a **mixed sequence**. The mixed sequence may be based on either a coordinate sequence or a subordinate sequence. Here are examples of each kind.

Mixed coordinate sequence

In this type of paragraph, the intent of the writer is to offer a series of examples or comments that develop the opening generality. Note the coordinate sequence of the three Level 2s. At any point, however, the writer may say more about a second-level element by going to a third or even deeper level. But the coordinate aspect still dominates.

1 I feel, therefore, that there is a close connection among three aspects of language in our society.

2 First is the associative squirrel-chatter that one hears on streets, and even in college halls, jerking along apologetically or defiantly in a series of unshaped phrases, using slang or vogue words for emphasis or punctuation.

2 Second is the poetic illiteracy which regards anything in verse as a verbal puzzle, not even as a puzzle to be worked out, but a distasteful and inscrutable puzzle without an answer.

2 Third is the dead, senseless, sentenceless, written pseudo-prose that surrounds us like a boa constrictor, which is said to cover its victims with slime before strangling them.

3 This last, under the names of jargon, gobbledygook, and the like, has often enough been recognized as a disease of contemporary language and ridiculed or deplored as such.

—Northrop Frye

Mixed subordinate sequence

In this kind of paragraph, the writer is steadily moving toward a very specific end, using the subordinate sequence (Levels 1, 2, 3, 4). Along the way, he or she may pause to develop a thought by using two or more coordinate elements (here, two Level 2s). The progression then resumes, however, and there will be no backtracking to previous levels. The subordinate pattern still dominates.

> 1   We have seen that the mind achieves freedom, once it is able to seek out meaning in experience.
>   2   But meaning is not confined to cause-and-effect relations in the physical world, nor, for that matter, to analyses of social behavior.
>   2   Nor is meaning confined to economic activities.
>   3   We do not grow roses merely to sell them, we do not form a collection of records just to study acoustics, we do not ask of every book we read: "How will this increase my efficiency at the office?"
>   4   Meaning has another dimension: the dimension of culture.
>
> —Howard Mumford Jones

Careful writing—in order to produce easy reading—requires us to pay attention to coordinate and subordinate elements. Remember that expository writing deals with abstract material, so we must give our readers all the help we can. Part of such help is to state ideas that are similar by using similar vocabulary and grammatical structures. When you move to an idea that is of a different level of generality, either higher or lower, you should try to signal that change to your reader by using different vocabulary and grammatical structures.

THE PARAGRAPH

Name:_____

EXERCISE E: mixed sequence–part 1

Accuracy _____ Creativity _____

Directions: Use the following sentences as base sentences to write paragraphs that show a mixed sequence. The first two should begin paragraphs based on the coordinate sequence. You must add at least three second-level elements (Level 2s), and to any or all of these you must add one or more subordinate sentences. For example, 1-2-3-2-2-3, or 1-2-3-2-3-4-2

Use your own paper for all four paragraphs.

1. The way a person speaks can tell us many things in addition to the message of the words themselves.

2. There are two kinds of manners, the formal manners that we are taught and the instinctive manners that arise from a concern for others.

These next two sentences should be used to begin paragraphs based on the subordinate sequence. To do this you must add three sentences using the sequence 2, 3, 4. Then you must add a second Level 2 (or Level 3 or Level 4), but maintain the subordinate, or downward, progression of the paragraph. For example, 1-2-3-3-4, or 1-2-2-3-4.

3. A vacation is often a turning point in a person's life.

4. Sometimes the information we've been searching so hard to find turns out to be far more than we ever wanted.

THE PARAGRAPH

Name:_____

EXERCISE F: mixed sequence–part 2

Accuracy _____ Creativity _____

Directions: The following quotations are to be used as the base for the opening sentence of a paragraph that has a mixed sequence—either mixed coordinate or mixed subordinate. You may agree or disagree with the author or express reservations about the statement. If you wish, you may use only part of the quotation. Because of the wide variety of paragraphs possible, a sample has not been provided. Use your own paper for this exercise.

1. "The superior man understands what is right; the inferior man understands what will sell."
    —Confucius

2. "One of the oldest human needs is having someone to wonder where you are when you don't come home at night."—Margaret Mead

3. "We are wrong if we think that the experience of loss is bad and to be avoided."
    —Helene Cixous

4. "The task of the educator lies in seeing that the child does not confound good with immobility and evil with activity."—Maria Montessori

5.   "The vocation of every man and woman is to serve other people."—Leo N. Tolstoi

6. "We seem headed for a standardization of the mind, what Goethe called the 'deadly commonplace that fetters us all.' "—Edith Hamilton

7. "I am convinced that the spontaneous judgment of the public is always more authentic than the opinion of those who set themselves up to be judges of works of art."—Igor Stravinsky

8. "Parents can only give good advice or put them on the right paths, but the final forming of a person's character lies in their own hands."—Anne Frank

9. "Man is a reservoir of indetermination; his power of choice for good or evil is enormous."
    —Henri Bergson

10. "There is no adequate defense, except stupidity, against a new idea."—Percy W. Bridgman

OTHER PARAGRAPH FORMS

The placement of the base, or topic, sentence at the beginning of a paragraph is by far the most common method used in expository writing. It alerts the reader to the subject matter about to be discussed, and often implies the sequence, simple or mixed, coordinate or subordinate, that will be followed.

But paragraphs are usually not found in isolation. More often, they are parts of a larger whole, an essay, a review, a biography, or any of the myriad other uses of expository prose. And during the course of that work, the author will often have to make a transition from one line of thinking to another or introduce a new topic or conclude an old one. The sentences required to achieve these purposes can be considered outside the structure of the paragraph itself but vital to the reader's complete understanding of the presentation. The following examples will illustrate these points.

Paragraph with transitional element

In this paragraph, the first sentence is *transitional* (T). The first half of the sentence refers to material previously covered—false ideas about poetry; the second half of the opening sentence introduces the topic, not of just this paragraph, but of the next sequence of paragraphs. Thus this transitional sentence swings the discussion from what poetry is not, to what it is.

The second sentence sets up a "straw man" argument that is demolished by the coordinate sequence that follows. Thus the second sentence (Level 1) is actually the topic sentence, the one on which the rest of the paragraph is a comment.

T We've got rid of some false ideas about poetry; but we still have to try and find out what *is* the use of it.

1 Now, in a way, to ask what is the use of poetry should be as absurd as asking what is the use of a rainbow, or the sea, or a piece of taffy, or a game of football, or a nice dress.

2 A rainbow is a natural phenomenon, the result of the refraction and reflection of the sun's rays in drops of rain.

3 As far as mankind is concerned, it's a perfectly useless object: it certainly won't help anyone to make money.

4 Yet the poet who said, "My heart leaps up when I behold a rainbow in the sky," only put into words the feeling of wonder and excitement we all have when we see a rainbow.

5 It is something beautiful in its own right, just like a good poem.

2 When you are given a piece of taffy, or a nice dress, you don't sit around wondering what is the use of it: you put the one into your mouth, or your head into the other.

2 You enjoy bathing in the sea on a hot day, or playing a game of football, in just the same way.

—C. Day Lewis

Paragraph with introductory element

In the next paragraph, the first two sentences are *introductory* (I). They explain the physical phenomenon of pitch as it would be explained in physics. But the paragraph is not about musical pitch in general; it is about the human voice. Thus the third sentence is the base sentence, to which the first two are introductory. Note the coordinate arrangement of the Level 3s.

I-1   Any musical tone has a pitch, which is determined by the fundamental frequency of vibration of the string, reed, column of air, metal or glass plate, or bell, or whatever it is that produces the tone.

I-2   The greater the number of vibrations per second, the higher the pitch.

    1   The human voice, produced by the vibrating vocal cords, also has pitch.

      2   Since we can change the rate of vibration of the vocal cords by varying the amount of tension with which they are contracted, we are capable of varying the pitch of the voice.

        3   In singing this is done in order to produce the musical effect of a melody.

        3   In speech it is done in order to produce the pitch contours which are a characteristic feature of phonological phrases.

          —W. Nelson Francis

Paragraph with concluding element

Properly used, a *concluding* element (C) can provide a summing up of the paragraph or give a satisfying sense of finality. Improperly used, it can be a superfluous or heavy-handed way to end an otherwise skillful presentation.

    In the following paragraph the authors are discussing the origin of the phrase "Mind your *P*'s and *Q*'s," and they end the paragraph with an apt literary quotation.

    1   In regard to its original meaning there has been much conjecture, with no really satisfying explanation.

      2   Some believe it was a warning of schoolteachers to those learning to write the alphabet or of master printers to their apprentices in setting type.

      2   Some think it has to do with *p*ints and *q*uarts in the alehouse reckoning.

      2   Some think it was an injunction of French dancing masters to their charges, to mind their feet (*pieds*) and pigtails or wigs (*queues*).

      2   And some would have solicitous wives beseeching their husbands, especially if they were seamen who often tarred their pigtails (*queues*), not to soil their *pea*jackets.

C   The interpretations of linguistic obscurities, as Chaucer once drily remarked, "is a glorious art, certeyn."

        —Bergen and Cornelia Evans

126

THE PARAGRAPH

Name:_____

EXERCISE G: other paragraph forms
—part 1

Accuracy _____ Creativity _____

Directions: Following is a list of quotations, each marked to be used as an introduction (I), transition (T), or conclusion (C). Build a paragraph around each quotation, using it in the manner suggested. Use your own paper for this exercise.

1. (I)   "The parts of a composition may be poetical, without the composition as a whole being a poem."—Percy Bysshe Shelley

2. (I)   "The cause of peace is not the cause of cowardice."—Ralph Waldo Emerson

3. (T)   "The one thing that doesn't abide by majority rule is a person's conscience."
—Harper Lee

4. (T)   "Yet panics, in some cases, have their uses; they produce as much good as hurt."
—Thomas Paine

5. (C)   "The world is round and the place which may seem like the end may also be only the beginning."—Ivy Baker Priest

6. (C)   "The difficult problems are the fundamental problems; simplicity stands at the end, not at the beginning of a work."—Anni Albers

THE PARAGRAPH

Name:_____

EXERCISE H: other paragraph forms
  –part 2

Accuracy _____ Creativity _____

Directions: Using all the techniques available to you, take each of the following quotations as the topic sentence for a paragraph, and develop it as skillfully as possible. Use your own paper for this exercise.

1. "It is remarkable how easily and insensibly we fall into a particular route, and make a beaten track for ourselves."—Henry David Thoreau

2. "We live by our imaginations, by our admirations, by our sentiments."
    —Ralph Waldo Emerson

3. "Art is long, life short, judgment difficult, opportunity transient."—Johann W. Goethe

CPSIA information can be obtained
at www.ICGtesting.com
Printed in the USA
LVHW011500010922
727308LV00008B/524